tactical, and strategic nuclear are analyzed. Finally, suggestions are given for improving the ability of the U.S. and NATO to cope with the threat of theatre or tactical nuclear warfare.

As the first thorough treatment of this subject, *Tactical Nuclear Weapons: An Examination of the Issues* is suitable for undergraduate and graduate courses in National Security Affairs, U.S. Defense Policy, NATO, U.S.-Soviet Relations, and Nuclear Weapons; and will be of interest to professionals and researchers involved in International Studies.

Dr. William R. Van Cleave is Professor and Director of Defense and Strategic Studies at the School of International Relations, University of Southern California. He has served as strategic analyst and consultant to public and private agencies including the Department of Defense. Dr. Van Cleave was also a member of the "B" Team on Competitive Intelligence Analysis 1976-1977.

S.T. Cohen, nuclear physicist, military analyst, and consultant on defense policy matters, is the "Father of the Neutron Bomb" and has been associated with tactical nuclear weapons for 25 years.

Tactical Nuclear Weapons

An Examination of the Issues

TACTICAL
Nuclear Weapons:

An Examination of the Issues

William R. Van Cleave and S.T. Cohen

Crane, Russak   New York

Tactical Nuclear Weapons
Published in the United States by
Crane, Russak & Company, Inc.
347 Madison Avenue
New York, New York 10017
ISBN 0-8448-1260-9
LC 77-83272

Printed in the United States of America

Table of Contents

Preface

In June 1976, a NATO ministerial meeting took place in Brussels where NATO's Nuclear Planning Group (NPG) agreed on the necessity of improving the overall effectiveness of its tactical nuclear weapons (TNW) capabilities. Special consideration was given to improvements in the survivability of NATO's TNW forces. The need to enhance the security of these weapons and the command, control, and communications affecting their use was also stated.

In connection with this expression of concern and interest in improving NATO's TNW capabilities, the NPG recently initiated studies of the military and political implications of advanced technologies related to improved tactical nuclear warheads, target acquisition, precision-guidance, and communications. However, the policy guidance behind these studies seems to have been cast in the mold of NATO's basic policy of flexible response, which evolved during the early 1960s and was officially accepted by NATO in 1967.

It should be realized that very substantial, and even profound, changes in the U.S.-NATO–Soviet-Warsaw Pact nuclear balance (both strategic and tactical) have taken place since the flexible response doctrine was formulated. So the question arises as to whether, in seeking technological solutions to acknowledged NATO TNW deficiencies, the full depth of the basic issues surrounding the problem is being realistically considered.

Thus far, in recent discussions of NATO TNW issues, what seems not to have received sufficient attention and discussion is the interrelationship of NATO's policy and posture, the nature of the threat, and *actual* tactical nuclear conflict—and, in that context, what the *requirements* for tactical nuclear weapons employment might be. Explicit doctrinal and planning criteria for tactical nuclear forces have not been set forth. Employment policies, to the extent they exist at all, are fuzzy at best, and serious military training by NATO for operations in a tactical nuclear conflict (with battlefield employment by one or both sides) is virtually nonexistent. TNW generally continue to be regarded more politically for their "escalatory" potential than militarily for defensive or war-fighting purposes.

Moreover, in the framework of NATO's current policy, what requirements exist for tactical nuclear weapons and other military forces in Europe are based upon a Western-defined (or Western-preferred) threat and a desire to avoid the use of nuclear weapons at nearly all costs. This has produced a planning presumption that major aggression against Western Europe will follow an identifiable preparation, will be at least initially nonnuclear, and might be kept nonnuclear pending a Western decision to introduce nuclear weapons into the conflict. However, given what we now believe we understand of Soviet TNW capabilities, doctrine, and operational planning, this may be a most unlikely case, in which event a very different assessment of NATO force requirements would be in order. It is to these matters that this discussion is addressed.

It is hardly necessary to point out that NATO's tactical nuclear weapons and policies have been, and continue to be, a subject of swirling uncertainty and confusion. Until recently, however, the great bulk of whatever controversy has been made public has been produced by Western scholars and analysts outside government. Few in the Soviet Union have chosen to join directly in the Western dialogue, although on occasion there is published Soviet commentary on that dialogue. There is also an increasing amount of Soviet military literature available in the West that may reveal Soviet thinking on nuclear matters far more accurately than Western planning assumptions.

In reaching for source material for this report we have chosen to dwell largely upon statements of Western and Soviet political and military officials in government or recently out of it so that our assessment may be reasonably consonant with the official situation.

Introduction

Based upon policy decisions made primarily in 1953 and 1954, the United States mounted a major effort during the 1950s to develop and produce nuclear weapons for tactical purposes and theater deployment. By the mid-1960s—even though U.S. doctrine had changed drastically from the nuclear emphasis underlying the decisions reached in 1953–54—some 7,000 warheads were reportedly deployed in the European theater and an undisclosed number in the Asian-Pacific area. This deployment has continued to the present, but its meaning and its military-political value have come into increasing question. Moreover, there is a mounting U.S. apprehensiveness over the physical security of those weapons deployed abroad. As a result, there are indications that congressional pressure (apparently not vigorously resisted by the executive branch) will result in withdrawals of certain tactical nuclear weapons and reductions in the number of those deployed overseas.

Until very recently, the deployment of tactical nuclear weapons and questions of when and how they might be used have been a subject of limited interest, and even more limited perspicacity, compared to the scope of intellectual activity on strategic nuclear issues. Whereas that community in the United States that concerns itself with national security has waxed frequently and eloquently on the strategic side, every so often stirring up major national debate and

1

concern, on the tactical side the relative paucity of public interest and intellectualization has produced no great debate and, it would appear, but little thought. This situation is also reflected in arms control attention, as for example in the current U.S. approach to a comprehensive ban or moratorium on nuclear testing, where the focus is on possible consequences for strategic nuclear capabilities rather than on the probability that the Soviets, under such arrangements, would have one-sided freedom to continue to improve their tactical nuclear warhead technology through unverifiable testing.

Recently, however, certain elements in the Congress (particularly in the Senate) have begun to probe into the tactical nuclear side. This activity came to a head with the adoption of the Nunn amendment (sponsored by Senator Sam Nunn, D-Georgia) to Public Law 93-365, on August 5, 1974 (the Department of Defense Appropriation Authorization Act, 1975), which directed the Secretary of Defense to "study the overall concept for use of tactical nuclear weapons in Europe; how the use of such weapons relates to deterrence and to a strong *conventional* defense; reduction in the number and type of nuclear warheads which are not essential for the defense structure for Western Europe; and the steps that can be taken to develop a rational and coordinated nuclear posture by the NATO alliance that is consistent with proper emphasis on *conventional* defense forces." (Emphasis added.)

By couching the study directive in the framework of conventional defense emphasis rather than a combined nuclear and nonnuclear environment, the Nunn amendment nearly precluded the possibility that the study could deal realistically with the issue of "overall concept for use," as related to actual warfighting operations, or how use relates to deterrence.

Nonetheless, Secretary Schlesinger's reply to the Nunn amendment directive[1] constituted a discussion and release of official information dealing with tactical nuclear weapon issues on a scale unprecedented in the history of the Office of the Secretary of Defense. For this reason alone, that report is highly recommended to those seeking relevant background material on those issues.

It is largely in view of such recent and continuing indications of a reawakened interest in NATO and in tactical nuclear issues that this attempt to address those issues is undertaken.

Background:
History of Tactical Nuclear Weapons Treatment

During the more than twenty years of U.S. development and deployment of tactical nuclear weapons (TNW), governmental attitudes and politics on the subject have shifted.

For several years into the nuclear age, there was little interest in, or support for, tactical use of nuclear weapons. In part, this was due to the limited early state of knowledge about nuclear technology and the inability to project the potential of these weapons.* For example, the eminent scientist Vannevar Bush wrote in 1949:

> The atomic bomb cannot be subdivided. This is inherent in the physics of the situation. . . . There will be no shells for guns carrying atomic explosives, nor will they be carried by marine torpedoes or small rockets or in any other retail way. Atomic bombs will be used only against important targets to which it pays to devote a large effort.[2]

In part it was due to a combination of technological infancy and military reluctance to consider the weapons in other than a "strategic" sense. Even when the Air Force was told at a postwar Los Alamos

---

*In the early 1950s, the U.S. Air Force assembled a group of prominent nuclear weapon experts, headed by Dr. John Von Neumann, which did make such projections. In particular, their forecast that megaton thermonuclear weapons could be developed in relatively small, light packages was a major impetus to the decision to accelerate the ICBM program.

3

meeting of the potential flexibility of the technology for weapons, its representatives responded, "The bomb we have now is precisely what we need."[3] And when the commandant of the Army Command and Staff College, Brigadier General Herbert Loper, directed the preparation of a manual for the possible use of nuclear weapons in combat, his instructions were, "Show me how to use this weapon tactically. It is *not* a tactical weapon."[4]

However, on the heels of technological advance and the Korean War, views began to change.

In seeking support in 1952 for a special $3 billion appropriations bill that would permit major tactical nuclear weapons endeavors by the U.S. Atomic Energy Commission (AEC), Gordon Dean, chairman of the AEC, stated:

> *The setting in which this request is made stems from recent revolutionary developments in the field of atomic weapons technology. Through these developments, the whole concept of how atomic weapons can be utilized in warfare has been radically revised. No longer are they to be used in a "Hiroshima-type" way against cities and industrial areas. It is now possible to have a complete "family" of atomic weapons for use not only by strategic bombers, but also by ground support aircraft, armies, and navies.*[5]

Somewhat more than two years later, when a number of nuclear weapons had been deployed to NATO Europe, the nuclear policies of the Eisenhower administration made it manifestly clear that major emphasis was placed on their actual combat use. In October 1953, President Eisenhower made official the nuclear emphasis policy recommended by NSC 162/2 Basic National Security Policy and directed the military to base planning on the use of nuclear weapons when the military situation required. A year later, this was adopted as NATO policy. In this vein, Secretary of State John Foster Dulles proclaimed:

> *The present policies will gradually involve the use of atomic weapons as conventional weapons for tactical purposes. If that occurs and there is a replacement of what is now known as conventional weapons by a different type of weapon, they will, of course, be used.*[6]

Views such as these generally dominated U.S. policies of the 1950s even after criticism of the Eisenhower policies began to grow. The reaction that grew was generally not against limited, tactical use of nuclear weapons but against "massive retaliation." However, by the end of the 1950s, a debate had developed over limited war forces, including the role of tactical nuclear weapons in limited war strategy.

It was the election of John F. Kennedy that caused an abrupt switch in the U.S. assessment of tactical nuclear weapons. General Maxwell Taylor's appeal for "flexible response" became translated into "conventional emphasis," and a concerted effort was made to build up U.S. and NATO nonnuclear military capabilities and to base limited war planning on them. As two senior officials of the Department of Defense later wrote:

> One of the first major policy changes sought by the Kennedy Administration in 1961 was to reduce the reliance on nuclear weapons for deterrence and defense and increase the reliance on conventional forces, especially in NATO.[7]

The change in national policy in 1961 was followed by an equally stark change in military training, interest, and doctrinal development. On the basis of the policy guidance of the Eisenhower administration, there had developed keen and innovative military interest in the nuclear battlefield, particularly in the army. By 1955, 50 percent of instruction and training at the army's Command and General Staff College (CGSC) was devoted to TNW battlefield situations. A study of the curriculum concluded that even that was not adequate training in TNW tactics and employment. Consequently, the U.S. Continental Army Command in 1956 directed the CGSC "to depict atomic warfare as the typical and to treat nonatomic warfare as modification of the typical" in training and exercises. The CGSC commandant's guidance for the 1957–58 course of instruction was that:

> the Atomic Era is upon us. . . . Accordingly, from the beginning we must teach the student to think, act, and react primarily in terms of an atomic environment on the battlefield. To accomplish the College mission, we must abandon outmoted concepts and procedures and replace them with fresh and forward-thinking approaches that recognize the realities of the present, and the future.

That year the Regular Course curriculum included 614 hours of nuclear-weapons instruction for the battlefield.[8]

The army, in the meantime, had adjusted organizationally to the atomic battlefield that it foresaw with the development of the "pentomic" division. And, as a study of the period by Major John P. Rose, U.S. Army, put it, "U. S. Army officers in the 1950s were most progressive to the notions of the atomic age. The weight of military writing during this time was clearly centered on the atomic battlefield."[9] During the eight years of the Eisenhower administration, from 1953 through 1960, the army's *Military Review* contained 155 articles dealing with TNW.

When the policies and preferences of the new administration became known in 1961, the military change was remarkably sudden. On 25 May 1961, President Kennedy directed that the army reorganize its divisional structure away from the pentomic division and the atomic battlefield toward an organization emphasizing nonnuclear operations. The Command and General Staff College adjusted its curriculum accordingly. The Senior Officer Nuclear Weapons Employment Course became the Senior Advanced Operations Course; the Department of Nuclear Weapons was abolished. Compared with the 614 annual hours of instruction on nuclear weapons in 1957–58, by the 1966–67 training year there were only 21 hours of "special weapons" instruction, which soon dropped to 16 hours. It was as if nuclear weapons had disappeared by fiat from military concern. During the eight years 1962 through 1969 *Military Review* carried only 26 articles dealing with TNW, compared with nearly 150 on guerrilla operations and such "unconventional" (now conventional) warfare.

The situation has continued to this day. In the eight years, 1970 through 1977, *Military Review* carried 13 articles on TNW. A 1973 study published in *Military Review* concluded that ". . . in the current instruction at the U.S. Army Command and General Staff College, active nuclear environments are the exception rather than the rule." As Major Rose concluded, concerning the Army and TNW, "If the 1950s can be characterized as an 'invitation to think,' then the 1960s certainly reflected stagnation in thinking." And as for today, "A close examination of published Army doctrine reveals a clear and strong emphasis directed toward combat operations on a conventional battlefield. The possibility of future nuclear land combat operations is largely avoided."[10]

It is ironical that the negative attitude toward tactical nuclear weapons hardened at the same time that technology was being developed to support a tactical nuclear emphasis doctrine far more reasonably and credibly than technology allowed during the days of tactical nuclear emphasis policy.

In September 1964 (reacting to statements made by presidential candidate Senator Barry Goldwater), President Johnson made explicit the reversal of the position taken by the Eisenhower administration, maintaining:

> *Make no mistake. There is no such thing as a conventional nuclear weapon. For 19 peril-filled years, no nation has loosed the atom against another. To do so now is a political decision of the highest order.*[11]

Today, the tactical nuclear policies of the Kennedy-Johnson years still prevail in that the distinction between conventional and nuclear weapons remains sharply drawn. U.S. reluctance to use tactical nuclear weapons clearly remains high. Former Secretary of Defense James R. Schlesinger stated officially a theme that he reiterated many times:

> *At the same time, I must stress that our tactical nuclear systems do not now and are most unlikely in the future to constitute a serious substitute for a stalwart non-nuclear defense. In fact, we must recognize in our planning that the decision to initiate the use of nuclear weapons—however small, clean, and precisely used they might be—would be the most agonizing that could face any national leader.*[12]

By law, the employment of U.S. tactical nuclear weapons can only take place after a release decision by the commander in chief, the president. In this connection, we might note that not since President Eisenhower has a president declared himself unequivocally, or even very clearly, as to his thoughts on the actual employment of tactical nuclear weapons.

John Kennedy's public utterances on defense matters excluded specific remarks on their use. However, he did intimate strongly that any use would produce only negative and even catastrophic results. The crossing of the nuclear firebreak was something to be avoided at almost any cost.

Lyndon Johnson's famous declaration during the 1964 campaign has been cited. Moreover, like Kennedy before him, none of President

Johnson's comments on nuclear weaponry ever contained a consideration of terms for use in local-limited conflict.

Richard Nixon, possibly sensing that the subject had been dusted under the carpet for too long, asked early in his administration a number of critical questions on the role of tactical nuclear weapons. The answers provided for his consideration have not been made public, but we do know that he continued the conventional emphasis policies of Kennedy and Johnson, and no decisions were made for any significant change in the U.S. tactical nuclear posture. Furthermore, President Nixon went one step beyond President Johnson's reluctance to define any potential role for TNW by specifically excluding certain use, declaring that under no conditions would he sanction TNW use in the Southeast Asian conflict.

TNW were not specifically included in Gerald Ford's remarks on military matters, except for an acknowledgment of TNW deployment in the Republic of Korea and of the possibility that they would be used if necessary.* And they have not, to date, been specifically addressed by President Carter, although many of his general remarks have indicated a desire to reduce even further reliance on nuclear weapons.

In providing his views to the Senate concerning appropriation of funds for the enhanced radiation warhead, however, President Carter reaffirmed the established Presidential onus on nuclear usage, explicitly applying it to nuclear weapons of *any* type:

> The decision to use nuclear weapons of any kind, including ER weapons, would remain in my hands, not in the hands of local theater commanders. A decision to cross the nuclear threshold would be the most agonizing decision to be made by any President. I can assure you that these weapons, i.e., low yield, enhanced radiation weapons, would not make that decision any easier.

At the same time, President Carter declared himself in favor of modernization of the TNW stockpile:

> We must retain and modernize our theater nuclear capabilities, especially in support of NATO's deterrent strategy of flexible response. Tactical nu-

---

*In affirming a previous statement by Secretary Schlesinger that U.S. TNW are deployed in the Republic of Korea and could be used in event of an invasion, President Ford said, "I am saying we have the forces and they will be used in our national interest." (June 25, 1975, press conference, quoted in "New U.S. Strategy for Nuclear War," *Washington Post*, July 21, 1975.)

> *clear weapons, including those for battlefield use, have strongly contrib-*
> *uted to deterrence of conflict in Europe. I believe we must retain the*
> *option they provide, and modernize it.*[13]

While the "most agonizing decision" part comes through clearly, indeed, there is little more than confusion concerning the employment of tactical nuclear weapons. At times, the initiative seems ceded to the enemy, and official statements approach a "no first use" tone in their emphasis on TNW employment only in response to enemy use; at other times—such as in NATO planning—it seems assumed that the U.S. will have first use in all cases, in staving off conventional defeat. Both the reluctance to use and the confusion concerning use is reflected in the official Army doctrinal manuals, such as the current guide, *The Army in the Field,* which states, "Unless the enemy uses them first, nuclear weapons will not be authorized . . ." to which the manual then adds:

> *. . . before conventional defenses have been severely tested and found*
> *inadequate. The situation facing corps at the time nuclear weapons are*
> *requested must therefore be grave—under sustained attack by superior*
> *forces, own forces becoming fully committed and not likely to hold, rein-*
> *forcements not available, insufficient combat support and combat service*
> *support available to sustain the defense, and the survivability of the force*
> *in question.*

It is fair to say that today the United States has a decided aversion to using TNW and, at best, a muddled policy embracing their role. The fact is that despite the development and growth of the technology, including the means of delivery, the U.S. military currently possesses no credible doctrine for TNW employment, particularly in a situation where the opponent may also employ such weapons. Overwhelmingly, official and scholarly views, as expressed in public, are highly negative on the subject of TNW policy. (Even those who see an important role in principle for these weapons see but a very limited role for the current stockpile.)

In a military sense there seems to have been very little progress since one of those instrumental in arguing for and catalyzing the early development of tactical nuclear weapons, J. Robert Oppenheimer, declared a quarter of a century ago:

I am not qualified, and if I were qualified I would not be allowed, to give a detailed evaluation of the appropriateness of the use of atomic weapons against any or all such (military) targets; but one thing is very clear. It is clear that they can be used only as adjuncts in a military campaign which has some other components, and whose purpose is a military victory. They are not primarily weapons of totality or terror, but weapons used to give combat forces help that they would otherwise lack. They are an integral part of military operations. Only when the atomic bomb is recognized as useful insofar as it is an integral part of military operations, will it really be of much help in the fighting of a war, rather than in warning all mankind to avert it.[14]

Dr. Oppenheimer's feelings about the potential of tactical nuclear weapons seem to be shared by neither U.S. policymakers nor military leaders. Admittedly, his viewpoint was given at a time when the world was different in many respects from what it is now; and many would argue that changes have invalidated Oppenheimer's beliefs. But there are others who feel that these beliefs hold even more truly now than before in view of the present strategic nuclear balance, U.S. difficulties in coping successfully with conventional conflict, and the apparent Soviet emphasis on preparing for nuclear warfare, which the West has not taken seriously.

In fact, the inadequacies of NATO's defensive posture are more severe at the present time than at any time since the introduction of the conventional emphasis doctrine. In contrast to the malaise that has inflicted NATO in recent years, the Soviet Union has made a major effort to improve Warsaw Pact nuclear and nonnuclear attack capabilities in the very ways most threatening to NATO's postural and planning weaknesses. A recent report to the Senate Committee on Armed Services by Senator Sam Nunn and Senator Dewey Bartlett (R-Oklahoma) concluded:

The Warsaw Pact forces which confront NATO today across the inter-German border represent more than simply an enlarged threat. It is a threat whose character has been deliberately re-tailored to exploit fully the very weaknesses in NATO's conventional posture which have always plagued the Alliance.

The report particularly emphasized the new capability of the Pact to launch a devastating assault without warning, in direct contradiction of NATO's major planning assumption of fairly long lead-time warning:

> *While Soviet forces in Eastern Europe can initiate a conflict from a standing start, NATO forces continue to require warning time of a duration sufficient to permit the Alliance to mobilize and deploy. . . . As the Warsaw Pact capability to attack from a standing start grows relative to NATO's defensive capacity, so does the likelihood that the Warsaw Pact would already be on the Rhine when the NATO decision is made to use tactical nuclear weapons.*[15]

It seems essential, then, to review NATO's posture and doctrine in comparison with that of the Warsaw Pact, and with particular attention given to the tactical nuclear component of the equation.

Tactical Nuclear Issues

Defining a tactical nuclear weapon is a thankless task, since to do so inevitably involves one's definition of tactical nuclear warfare; and, to date, a commonly accepted definition does not exist. The matter of the use of these weapons has been, and remains, intellectually and militarily fractured, with unreconciled bodies of opinion—ranging from contemplating the employment of a few weapons for demonstration of nuclear resolve to forecasting conflicts involving large-scale, theater-wide nuclear operations ending only at some unpredictable time later. With such extreme variations of opinion, it seems virtually impossible to define which systems' characteristics are critical to a tactical nuclear capability and what distinguishes TNW weapons and operations from non-TNW.

Determining the distinction between *tactical* and *strategic* or non-tactical can take on the character of a theological debate. But if one admits at the outset to numerous ambiguities wherein sharply drawn distinctions may not be possible, it is possible to clarify the terms sufficiently. There are several ways one may go about doing this. One could turn to the official Department of Defense dictionary of military terms, JCS, Pub. One. Here one finds that rather than defining tactical and strategic weapons the key distinction is that of *use*—purpose and effect, or, respectively, employment and mission:

> *Tactical Nuclear Weapons Employment: The use of nuclear weapons by land, sea, or air forces against opposing forces, supporting installations or*

13

facilities, in support of operations which contribute to the accomplishment of a military mission of limited scope or in support of the military commander's scheme of maneuver, usually limited to the area of military operations.

Strategic Mission: A mission directed against one or more of a selected series of enemy targets with the purpose of progressive destruction and disintegration of the enemy's war making capacity and his will to make war. . . . As opposed to tactical operations, strategic operations are designed to have a long-range, rather than an immediate, effect on the enemy and his military forces.[16]

These definitions themselves contain ambiguities and weaknesses; for example, the strategic definition rules out both immediate effects and limited strategic operations; and "supporting" and "usually" in the tactical definition may broaden it too much. Still, they serve as a useful starting point. The key consideration is clearly use. By itself, however, that might be insufficient inasmuch as an ICBM or B-52 or Poseidon might be used within the definition of *TNW employment.* And while it is difficult to imagine, with any common sense, an ADM (atomic demolition munition) or AFAP (artillery fired atomic projectile) being used within the *strategic missions* definition, it is conceivable.

While not denying these logical definitional problems, or the flexibility of use of various weapons, the TNW employment definition is acceptable with some qualification. First, the "usually" and "supporting installations or facilities" may be acceptable in defining *theater* nuclear weapons and operations, but they are inadequate for *tactical.* For any rigor, the term *tactical nuclear weapons* should be confined to those used in the immediate zone of military operations in a localized conflict away from American or Soviet soil, with great care—and reluctance—about applying the term to strikes against "supporting installations or facilities."

Second, in addition to use, there should be consideration of deployment, range, and yield, despite their shortcomings when considered separately. Tactical or theater nuclear weapons are those deployed *in* the theater, and, for the first, in the immediate area of combat for the above purposes. Their ranges and yields generally would be consistent with this use and deployment, that is, relatively short and low. Therefore, while an ICBM or SLBM could be employed in a theater conflict role, or even for tactical purposes, they are in no sense of the term tactical nuclear weapons.

In short, the term tactical nuclear weapons in the closest approximation refers to battlefield nuclear weapons, for battlefield use, and with deployment, ranges, and yields consistent with such use and confined essentially in each respect to the area of localized military operations. Admittedly, this description also leaves logically vulnerable points, but it suffices for the purposes of this paper. A complementary approach to differentiating *tactical* and *strategic* might be simply to see what specific systems the Department of Defense categorizes as strategic nuclear forces and which it categorizes as theater nuclear forces or nuclear general purpose forces. However, it should again be recognized that *theater nuclear forces* is the more encompassing term and *tactical nuclear forces* the more restrictive. It might be said that the United States has some 7,000 nuclear warheads in the NATO theater but not 7,000 *tactical* nuclear warheads, since many have range, delivery, and yield characteristics and are assigned missions that do not fit the above description. Supreme Allied Commander, Europe (SACEUR) once referred to about 3,000 tactical or battlefield weapons. Following this distinction, we do not include theater forces such as the Poseidon assigned to SACEUR, Pershing, and certain USAF aircraft, particularly those assigned to Quick Reaction Alert (QRA), in the term *tactical nuclear weapons* as used here. When those systems are included, the term *theater nuclear weapons* will be used.

The point is that we have in the European theater many assorted nuclear warheads and delivery systems, which are loosely—and improperly—referred to as tactical nuclear weapons. We also have weapons specifically deployed for tactical nuclear missions, as defined, that have physical properties so undesirable for tactical or battlefield purposes that calling them tactical nuclear weapons is inappropriate and virtually senseless. The mix of the existing inventory of theater and "tactical" nuclear weapons—as well as the inadequate doctrine, posture, and training for their use—is a major issue addressed in this paper.

However, these warheads and their delivery systems (certain of which would be next to useless were they relegated to high explosive payloads) remain, and the question of what to do with this uncertain investment remains nagging. Considering how these weapons are physically deployed in Europe—that is, in a limited number of storage sites highly vulnerable to attack and destruction—and how uncertain the conditions are for their employment, it has been argued that NATO might even be better off without most of them. Not only does their use seem improbable, it is argued, but they could invite an enemy preemptive attack. Exacerbating the problem are the age, technological dormancy, and consequent questionable effectiveness of many, or even most, of the warheads and delivery systems.

Apart from the warhead in the Lance surface-to-surface missile, which was itself configured well over a decade ago, and possibly the warhead in the Walleye air-to-surface missile, the nuclear technology in the U.S. tactical nuclear stockpile is essentially a product of the 1950s. Moreover, it should be realized that the progress made during the fifties, as impressive as it was, still represented only nuclear engineering improvements over the principles that were discovered during the late forties. The introduction of the Lance in 1974 and the Walleye ASM in 1972 has done nothing to change the basic situation. The progress that has been made in developing clean, tailored effects-weapons technology and highly discriminate warheads has not been reflected by actual progress in deployed weapons. As reflected by the current stockpile, this "new" technology has remained wholly unexploited—for so long, in fact, that it would be inappropriate now to refer to it as new. The average yield of the tactical nuclear warheads deployed may have gone down substantially (to less than 4 kilotons according to Secretary Schlesinger), since Secretary McNamara cited an average a few times that of the Hiroshima bomb; but however much that is an improvement, the technology has differed little.

As the deputy assistant administrator for national security of the Energy Research and Development Agency (ERDA) recently pointed out, with reference, as was later revealed, to an enhanced radiation (ER) warhead, "The new eight-inch shell will be the *first* U.S. weapon specially designed to reduce collateral damage from blast and radioactivity."[17] (Emphasis added.)

Moreover, in addition to confusion regarding their respective utility, the current inventory of delivery systems is also largely aged and even ancient. The Honest John rocket represents a technology now more than twenty years old. The Sergeant missile, soon to be retired, is not much younger. The F-4 aircraft, which carries the bulk of NATO's tactical atomic bombs, represents the state of the art of the late 1950s. Even the Lance missile, which after much delay is finally entering the NATO inventory, represents a design stage of well over a decade ago.

It would be incorrect to ascribe this technological stagnation to neglect. Rather than neglect, one could more appropriately say that it has been the result in part of continued indecisiveness as to what use to make of these weapons, and in part of an antipathy to such weapons and to their possible use, both of which have resulted in deliberate self-denial of the fruits of technology. As one analyst, who later became Secretary of Defense, concluded in a 1967 report:

> *The government has refrained from making certain investments in the capabilities for low-level nuclear warfare, not only because of the expense but because the creation of the options might tempt us to go through the firebreak, and would certainly give others the impression that we were willing to do so. . . . [This] represents deliberate exclusion through a self-denying ordinance of a whole range of options.*[18]

In the face of all this, there is a new and critical interest in U.S. tactical nuclear policies. In the past two or three years, for the first time, congressional committees in addition to the Joint Committee on Atomic Energy have held hearings, sponsored staff reports, and taken a major (although largely negative) interest. There has been a large number of articles published, compared to the preceding decade, and even fairly substantial newspaper coverage. While much of this has been generated by the publicity and debate over the "neutron bomb," or the proposed ER warhead, it also reflects a new and more general interest.

One of the consequences of this awakened interest and new questioning is that rationalization of U.S. tactical nuclear weapons programs, policies, and deployments—to Congress, to the public, and to allies—has become of increased importance. Yet, a clear-cut official rationale is very difficult to discern. Official statements about the use of tactical nuclear weapons—in curious contrast to rather definitive recent statements about uses of strategic nuclear weapons—are unsure and confusing. Recent annual Department of Defense reports are illustrative of this.

For example, in the FY 1975 Report, in contrast with some twenty pages of theorizing about strategic nuclear war and the controlled use of strategic nuclear weapons against the homeland of the USSR, tactical nuclear warfare and weapons are treated in no more than a page that leaves considerable doubt about their use. Compare:

Strategic Nuclear	*Tactical Nuclear*
. . . the principal features that we propose to maintain and improve in our strategic posture . . . are: . . . the forces to execute a wide range of options in response to potential actions by an enemy, including a capability for precise attacks on both soft and hard targets, while at the same time minimizing unintended collateral damage. (page 44)	*. . . as a practical matter, the initiation of a nuclear engagement would involve many uncertainties. Acceptable boundaries on such a conflict would be extremely difficult to establish. A nuclear engagement in the theater could well produce much higher military and civilian casualties and more widespread collateral damage than its non-nuclear counterpart. . . .*
To the extent that we have selective response options—smaller and more precisely focused than in the past—we should be able to deter. . . . But if deterrence fails, we may be able to bring all but the largest nuclear conflicts to a rapid conclusion before cities are struck. Damage may thus be limited and further escalation avoided. (page 38)	*What is more, it is not clear under what conditions the United States and its allies would possess a comparative military advantage in a tactical nuclear exchange.*
The availability of carefully tailored, pre-planned options will contribute to that end. They do not invite nuclear war; they discourage it. (page 42)	*. . . we must recognize in our planning that the decision to initiate the use of nuclear weapons—however small, clean, and precisely used they might be—would be the most agonizing that could face any national leader.*[19] (page 82)

The impression conveyed in the Department of Defense report is that strategic nuclear exchanges with the USSR can be controlled and should be planned for, while tactical use of nuclear weapons (on non-U.S. and non-USSR territory) cannot be; that it is possible to establish clear enough limitations in striking the USSR to justify a large number of strategic options and the capabilities to carry them out, but not apparently for tactical nuclear warfare; that it is possible to be very discriminate and to reduce collateral damage meaningfully, while carefully controlling escalation, in a strategic nuclear exchange, but not in the tactical use of nuclear weapons. In short, one gets the impression from reading the FY 1975 Department of Defense report of controlled and controllable strategic nuclear war and of uncontrollable tactical nuclear war. As the report says, "Acceptable boundaries on such a conflict [tactical nuclear] would be extremely difficult to establish."[20] An admonition that does not appear in the section on strategic nuclear war.

The FY 1977 Department of Defense report went a little farther concerning both the threat and specifically needed improvements in U.S. TNW in Europe. However, it too, despite some specificity on modernization, reflected only a vague and muddled employment concept—far from being doctrine—and was again explicit about an overriding reluctance to use the weapons or to base a defensive deterrent posture on them. Despite characterizing the Soviet-Pact threat as quintessentially nuclear in nature,* planning of general purpose forces for Europe remained curiously based upon the premise of nonnuclear attack and the report gratuitously singled out for disapproval those who would support a TNW emphasis policy against serious military threats. The report says:

> However tempting this view, *and the lower defense budgets that it might promise, it is an illusion. Quite apart from the dangers of escalation once the nuclear threshold has been crossed, the collateral damage that could accompany all but the most limited nuclear exchanges, the uncertain but no doubt extraordinary political effects that would follow any further use of nuclear weapons, and the gravity of the decision to authorize their use, nuclear weapons do not particularly exploit basic Western strengths.*[21]

Secretary Rumsfeld's last Department of Defense report (FY 1978) —its preparation was not begun under his predecessor as the preparation for FY 1977 had been—reflected a somewhat different tone and more specificity as to needed TNW improvements, while remaining

---

*"Doctrine and exercises indicate that the Warsaw Pact places high value on tactical surprise with nuclear weapons. . . . Warsaw Pact armored forces and their immediate support (artillery, tactical air, SAMs) are postured and trained to exploit nuclear attacks. . . . Warsaw Pact forces are postured primarily for the type of theater-wide nuclear strikes pictured in their doctrine and exercises." (p. 101)

conventional in emphasis. Perhaps reflecting a change, this report chose not to single out and emphasize uncertainties of tactical nuclear conflict; rather it applied to theater nuclear forces the same criteria used for strategic nuclear forces and specified required improvements in TNW in view of the growing Soviet nuclear threat:

> *We can be no less stringent in the demands on the theater nuclear forces. They too must be capable of riding out a surprise attack in sufficient numbers to execute a variety of theater-related plans. They too must be designed to minimize unnecessary collateral damage. They too must permit appropriate responses.*[22]

The report did not, however, go beyond the statement of such desiderata to clarify doctrine or employment concepts.

While the FY 1978 report is to some extent an exception, annual Department of Defense reports tend to set forth relatively clear planning criteria for strategic nuclear forces in contrast to tactical nuclear forces, and certainly a clearer rationale (however debatable it may remain) for evaluating the sufficiency and modernization of strategic forces than for theater-tactical nuclear forces. Uncertainty as to the role of TNW, coupled with vague and confused force planning assumptions that increase this uncertainty, make it very difficult to assess the reasonableness of today's tactical nuclear posture or tomorrow's TNW programs. Planning guidance on the relative roles and capabilities of conventional and tactical nuclear forces (or, for that matter, tactical and strategic nuclear forces in the theater)—despite an official emphasis on conventional defense against nonnuclear threats—is not very clear at this time. As the FY 1978 Department of Defense report acknowledged, "The current planning approach still does not come to grips adequately with an emerging nuclear problem." (p. 55) Because of that, it has been most difficult to answer critics and to explain or justify current weapons and new programs for "modernization."

What is our rationale for modernization? Are tactical nuclear weapons to deter by military effectiveness and defensive capability or principally by the threat of punishment and escalation? What are they to deter? When and how are they to be used?

The major U.S. planning assumption for theater forces is that an attack (e.g., a Warsaw Pact attack on Western Europe), however large and determined, will be nonnuclear and will be met by nonnuclear means—again, however large and determined. While it is expected that protracted nonnuclear conflict will result until a stalemate is reached and the situation is "stabilized," the use of TNW is not precluded and some sort of use seems envisaged should the nonnuclear defense clearly fail. In fact, presumably such first use rests with the West. Such a planning scenario obviously provides little guidance by which the deployment, role, or preferred characteristics of tactical nuclear weapons can be evaluated.

It seems strange that even though the consequences of strategic nuclear war between the United States and the USSR could be infinitely more dire for the United States than whatever might occur from tactical nuclear conflict fought in someone else's territory, there has been no reluctance whatsoever on the part of U.S. administrations to discuss the role of strategic weapons and to argue in strong terms for modernization and for the development of new systems. That a real threat exists that could result in a nuclear attack on the United States unless stringent measures were taken has been widely discussed and generally accepted by the United States for planning purposes; and the survivability of strategic forces in a scenario of a deliberate surprise disarming attack against them has received much more attention and concern than the survivability of theater nuclear forces against such an attack.

In order to ensure the survivability of strategic weapons, a top U.S. national priority has for many years been given to programs designed to reduce the vulnerability of these weapons to enemy nuclear attack. To this end, the Kennedy and Johnson administrations moved ahead on hardening land-based missile systems and expanding our nuclear submarine ballistic missile capabilities. The Nixon administration attempted to install a missile defense system to protect the land-based strategic deterrent, for which the president personally appealed to the American people in a nationwide TV address.

On the tactical side of the ledger, however, no comparable attention has been given to the survivability of U.S. nuclear weapons deployed outside the country, and little of real significance has been done to reduce their vulnerability to attack. This is particularly true with respect to surprise attacks. This continued reluctance has led to a situation in NATO where U.S. tactical nuclear policy is now at odds with itself. Whereas, on one hand, this policy holds that the fundamental role for tactical nuclear weapons in Europe is to deter nuclear attack on NATO, on the other hand, the high vulnerability of these weapons gives scant comfort that this alleged deterrent is at all credible; and, in fact, it can be argued—as one well-known pundit pointed out a decade ago—that this vulnerability gives every incentive to the Soviets to attack these forces with nuclear weapons in order to eliminate the possibility of an effective nuclear response:

> *Considering the extreme vulnerability of the tactical nuclear establishment on the Continent and the fact that the Soviets would not attack without expecting to win. . . . If there is large-scale aggression . . . the Soviets have every incentive to neutralize NATO's nuclear arsenal by launching an attack against it.*[23]

If there is any best way to ensure the nonuse of tactical nuclear weapons, it is to ensure that they won't be around to be used. In Western Europe, in a sense, the United States seems to be passing the buck to the Soviets on the nonuse problem by giving them the option to guarantee nonuse of NATO's weapons through preemptive nuclear attack. To allow U.S. strategic weapons, or any substantial component of them, to be placed in such a situation would obviously be deemed intolerable.

U.S. administrations have frequently sounded the tocsin regarding Soviet development of strategic nuclear weapons over the years; however, until very recently, very little has been said about the development and amassment of Soviet theater-tactical nuclear weapons and practically nothing about the threat they pose to NATO. For years the American public has been given official analyses of the U.S.-USSR strategic balance, with warnings of dire consequences should the Soviet buildup reach certain levels vis-à-vis those of the United States. In the area of the U.S.-USSR tactical nuclear balance and its implications for NATO security, however, we have had scarcely even an official mention, let alone an analysis, presented for national scrutiny. Yet, this dearth of attention in the United States has coincided with a substantial Soviet tactical nuclear buildup with increasing theater deployment.

For the first time, this was officially acknowledged by the Secretary of Defense in the annual Defense Report for FY 1976. In an unprecedented statement, the secretary reported: "But however much the original initiative lay with us, the Soviet Union has shown the liveliest possible interest in the concept of theater nuclear warfare. As a consequence, it is now the Soviets who set the pace here. . . ."[24]

This statement probably was made partly to balance the one-sided emphasis on U.S. theater nuclear weapons by the Soviets' "forward-based systems" argument in SALT and by arms control interests in the United States and partly to draw some attention to a neglected development. It is, nonetheless, true and therefore shows the need for some serious rethinking of NATO's defensive capabilities. It is no longer possible to concede theater nuclear superiority in Europe to NATO over the Warsaw Pact, as was pointed out by the director of the U.S. Arms Control and Disarmament Agency, who termed the theater nuclear balance "strongly in favor of the Soviet Union."[25]

In terms of weaponry involved, if the Soviets are conceded the offensive initiative, a substantial imbalance in favor of the Soviets has resulted, which further aggravates the vulnerability of NATO forces. In this respect, it is pointless simply to compare numbers of nuclear warheads and weapons in the theater and conclude that NATO has superiority by dint of its 7,000 to a frequently estimated (guessed) 3,500 Soviet nuclear warheads.* One of many reasons this is so is that we do *not know* the relevant numbers for the Warsaw Pact or which systems to include in the comparisons; whether or not, for example, to include weapons and warheads that are in the USSR but are still capable of early or even immediate employment in the theater. This approach also implies that the low-yield, short-range atomic artillery projectiles that constitute much of the NATO European stockpile are comparable one-to-one to the greater Soviet Scud-FROG-aircraft nuclear strike capability. But more important is the neglect in such comparisons of the unequal seriousness with which the two sides have regarded and prepared for nuclear conflict, and the possible effects of a Soviet counternuclear first strike.

---

*Professor John Erickson, in contrast, suggests that the number of Soviet nuclear warheads in this theater has been essentially doubled in recent years and now approximates the 7,000 attributed to NATO. ("Soviet Military Capabilities in Europe," *Journal of the Royal United Services Institute for Defense Studies* 120 [March 1975], p. 67.

American and Allied forces are ill-prepared and fundamentally un-trained for nuclear combat. Serious training of U.S. forces in Europe for a nuclear conflict environment ranges from no less than comical to nonexistent. In contrast, the Soviets have taken tactical nuclear con-flict very seriously, have trained their forces extensively for it, and have developed and deployed new classes of nuclear rockets and missiles for which doctrine and an offensive operational strategy apparently exist. To quote the Soviet minister of defense on this matter:

> *The operational and tactical missile units comprise the basis for the firepower of the Ground Troops. This is a qualitatively new branch of arms which is the basic means for employing nuclear weapons in combat and operations. The missile troops are capable of hitting any targets lo-cated at ranges of from several score to many hundreds of kilometers with great accuracy and dependability, using nuclear ammunition. As a result of the nuclear strikes, entire enemy subunits and units as well as different important objectives located in the enemy rear can be instantaneously wiped out. In terms of their combat properties, the missiles of our Ground Troops are not only not inferior to the foreign ones, but surpass them in terms of a number of important indexes.*[26]

Or to quote what is in essence the Soviet officers' manual for con-temporary offensive doctrine, which the Pentagon's response to the Nunn amendment singles out for citation:

> *Troops attacking in a different way will overcome the enemy's defense, not by "gnawing through" on narrow sectors and a solid front as was the case in past wars, but simultaneously across a broad front, along axes, from the march, at high tempos, right after nuclear strikes. . . .*[27]

These remarks, plus many others of a similar nature to be found in recent Soviet literature, are strongly indicative of the probability that the Soviet Union has chosen to regard tactical nuclear weapons as an acceptable and even principal means for the conduct of ground war-fare. In the United States, however, the opposite viewpoint has pre-vailed for some time. Consequently, the conclusion that Western forces are not trained or prepared for the real threat is ineluctable.* Moreover,

---

*The new Army FM 100-5 Field Manual, *Operations* (Department of the Army, July 1976), upon which all other Army "how to fight" manuals are based, does not even address the role of TNW in offensive or defensive operations. As Major Rose's study concluded: "FM 100-5 reflects the clear indication that future war will occur on a conventional battlefield and, for all practical purposes, avoids the possibility of future nuclear land combat operations." (Rose, "U.S. Army Doctrinal Developments.")

with respect to the Soviet nuclear threat to NATO, many beholders have ignored, denied, or disparaged it on the basis largely of their own intellectual mirror-images. Despite all the evidence of Soviet activity in this area, known Soviet views and capabilities all too often have been dismissed. Instead our own preferences and preferred strategy have been ascribed to the USSR, and the dialogue of NATO planning has been between its own assumptions and their projected mirror-image. The beholder has not scrutinized the Soviet side but has merely beheld himself in the mirror.*

Aside from the assessments of external beholders, the Soviets do have their own tactical nuclear options. What they are and what they may be in the future may remain a matter of controversy in the West. However, if the Soviet options are essentially in accord with those appearing in their own military literature and once suggested by Henry Kissinger, the policies now governing the U.S. view of tactical nuclear weapons would be subject to the most serious question.

In the following discussion of tactical nuclear issues, an effort will be made to present and analyze alternative views and interpretations. Which of these viewpoints are closer to the "truth" than others must be left to the reader's judgment and preferences. That so many uncertainties do exist, and that the basic issues are matters of judgment, means that categorical "truths" are impossible to establish. There are a number of critical imponderables having to do with tactical nuclear warfare that will leave it an issue poorly understood and largely unresolvable.†

---

*Again, verification of this can be found in army training. Recent Command and General Staff College lesson plans, entitled "Seeing the Battlefield" pose battlefield situations where nuclear weapons are not used by the enemy (or by the United States) even though the enemy is explicitly given that capability. The reasons for his abstinence are given as "political pressures, the threat of economic sanctions [sic], and the possibility of nuclear escalation."

†This does not suggest that it is fundamentally different from any other type of war, from Vietnam to strategic nuclear war, in this respect. One of the characteristics of many antinuclear discussions of tactical nuclear war is to compare the uncertainty and complexity of a postulated tactical nuclear war with the allegedly simple and clear rules and boundaries of other warfare. For example, two previously high level officials skeptical of TNW have asserted the following:

"The rules of a limited nuclear war would be complex and unclear. . . . In conventional war the rules are comparatively simple and clear.

"Conceivably, favorable and meaningful military results could be achieved with conventional forces; using tactical nuclear forces, by contrast, represented entry into an area in which we had had no prior combat experience and which involved such major uncertainty concerning the behavior of troops, civilians, and governments as to offer only low confidence of a favorable outcome." (Enthoven and Smith, *How Much Is Enough?* pp. 127, 130)

To put the last quotation in perspective, the reader might simply substitute *Vietnam* for the phrase, "using tactical nuclear forces."

On the other hand, there are those who, seemingly, have grappled with these imponderables and to their own satisfaction have reached firm conclusions that simply reject tactical nuclear capabilities and threats. The trouble, however, is that much of this conclusiveness has rested on highly subjective assumptions and preferences—political, military, and technological—that may have little or no basis in fact. In effect, these assumptions and the concomitant conclusions have led more to the creation of a mythology rather than a solid platform for U.S. policy formulation.

Knowns and Unknowns
in Tactical Nuclear Warfare

Political changes, internationally and domestically, have produced significant shifts in the evaluation of TNW and tactical nuclear warfare; technological changes have had less effect on such evaluation. Thus, over the years we have seen broad fluctuations in the official views and policy of the United States related to the role and utility of these weapons mostly as a consequence of political changes in the United States, but largely unrelated to the actual state of the technology and indistinctly related to military requirements.

Because of this, it is not at all clear that policies (or, in the case of individual spokesmen, recommended policies) have been consistent with either an objective analysis or a correct perception of the factors and alternatives involved. This is not to suggest that these positions were demonstrably or clearly wrong, however one views right and wrong in this area. So contentious and complex a matter is obviously judged largely in subjective fashion. What can be acknowledged, however, is that the rationale for policy and the reasons for shifts in policy have not always been well grounded, objective, or the product of overwhelmingly compelling analysis. There are strong indicators that many of the "careful studies" and "objective analyses" conducted during the 1960s in the Defense Department (e.g., by the Office of Systems

Analysis), that "showed" the wisdom of conventional emphasis and the disutility of tactical nuclear weapons for defense, came *after* the determination—subjectively made—that this should be so.* In fact, it is of interest to note that for a number of those who expressed themselves forcefully on tactical nuclear matters a dozen or more years ago, the passage of time and accompanying change have had no significant effect on their views.

Intellectually, then, the issues remain, with remarkably constant opposing schools of thought convinced of the correctness of their respective positions, while the relative validity of the contested positions remains unresolved. Since the core of most of these positions rests largely on unknowns and judgments concerning uncertain political and military factors, lack of resolution is likely to remain a permanent fixture. Positions are fashioned not on the basis of axioms but on assumptions, many quite arbitrary: and if the theorem is worked out with logic and consistency, the conclusions stem essentially from these assumptions. As you assume, so shall you derive your answers.

In working out a personal theorem on tactical nuclear issues, one should strive to include all relevant and (where possible) factual information in three areas. In decreasing order of factuality but increasing order of relevance for policy, these are: the technical, the military, and the political. In each, there are issues and associated unknowns to be examined.

Tactical Nuclear Weapons Technology

When the United States first deployed its so-called tactical nuclear weapons to Europe in the mid-1950s, they were viewed, in effect, as an adjunct to the punitively intended strategic capabilities of that period. The first systems introduced in England were the longer-ranged tactical aircraft—fighter bombers and medium bombers—designed for strikes deep into Eastern Europe and even the USSR. Even when the shorter-range battlefield systems were brought in later on, it was understood that this situation would not be changed by the introduction of such weapons to support NATO's conventional forces in forward

*Compare, for example, the statement by Enthoven and Smith cited earlier, which opened their chapter on NATO forces and strategy: "One of the first major policy changes *sought* . . . *in 1961*" (Emphasis added.) (Enthoven and Smith, *How Much Is Enough?*, p. 117.)

defense. It was anticipated that there would be only minimum use of these weapons (whose warhead yield averaged substantially in excess of the Hiroshima and Nagasaki bombs) on NATO territory; the nuclear destruction would be essentially limited to enemy forces and territory.

During the late 1950s, when the Soviets began deploying their own tactical nuclear systems (rockets and missiles) in Eastern Europe—much earlier than had been anticipated in the West—the utility of NATO's tactical nuclear doctrine began to erode. At this time, it became increasingly clear that tactical nuclear warfare would involve the forces and territories of both sides. However, the solution to this dilemma was not to work out a credible doctrine for NATO's tactical nuclear forces but to propound a new conventional emphasis doctrine that essentially relegated tactical nuclear weapons to a role of secondary importance (and somewhat paradoxically, given the changed situation, more as an escalatory threat than a means of territorial defense).

When, in the early 1960s, conventional emphasis became official U.S. policy, with NATO Europe only very reluctantly going along, the tactical nuclear weapons were left dangling, loosely attached to an amorphous doctrine. Ironically, it was at about this time that a "breakthrough" in discriminate warhead technology took place in the U.S. AEC laboratories, providing an opportunity to ameliorate the problem of civilian collateral damage through nuclear defense. Had U.S.-NATO policy not moved away from its nuclear emphasis doctrine, the contributions of discriminate nuclear warheads and their associated delivery systems would probably have come into sharper focus.

There are three aspects of tactical nuclear weapons technology that are most germane to assessment and resolution of the overall military issue: (1) U.S. warhead technology where, for many years, contradictory claims have been made not only about our ability to develop effective discriminate warheads but on their utility and desirability as well; (2) USSR warhead technology where, again, for many years conflicting opinions on the Soviet tactical nuclear stockpile have existed; and (3) the net technical assessment of United States versus USSR tactical nuclear weapons systems where, still again, there have been differences of opinion over the relative capabilities of each side.

U.S. Warhead Technology

> *Nuclear weapons, even in the lower kiloton ranges, are extremely de-structive devices and hardly the preferred weapons to defend such heavily populated areas as Europe.*[28] *(Robert S. McNamara)*

Such remarks are representative of a body of opinion that nuclear weapons, even of lower yields, are inherently highly destructive; and that as a consequence, the prospects for discriminate application (e.g., in NATO Europe) are remote. Yet, well before McNamara became secretary of defense, others emphasized the discriminate potential of nuclear weapons through which major collateral damage could be avoided. For example, John Foster Dulles stated almost twenty years ago:

> *The resourcefulness of those who serve our nation in the field of science and weapon engineering now shows that it is possible to alter the charac-ter of nuclear weapons. It seems now that their use need not involve vast destruction and widespread harm to humanity. Recent tests point to the possibility of possessing nuclear weapons, the destructiveness and radia-tion effects of which can be confined substantially to predetermined targets.*[29]

Thus, we note almost diametrically opposed views in the past re-garding prospects for discriminate tactical weapons. However, and this would hold true even were the full extent of opinion given on this issue to be set forth, on both sides of the argument what exactly is meant by "discriminate" or "vast destruction" is never spelled out. Without clearer standards for comparison, what can one make of such gross differences of opinion on discriminate capabilities?*

*The same problem exists in discussions of collateral damage from more or less limited attacks on the strategic level. See, for example, recent testimony of the Secretary of Defense wherein collateral damage, both short- and long-term, is analyzed incrementally for a range of attacks on the United States, U.S., Congress, Senate, Committee on Foreign Relations, *Briefing on Counterforce Attacks, Hearing* before the Subcommittee on Arms Control, International Law and Organization, 93rd Cong., 2nd sess., 1974. (Secret Hearing held September 11, 1974, made public January 10, 1975.) If the analysis given by the Secretary of Defense be allowed, it would appear that collateral damage from even major attacks on the United States, if restricted to strategic military targets, could be extremely limited as compared to the usual images of destruction; for example, less than one million fatalities from a one-thousand-megaton attack on *all* U.S. ICBMs, or about 300,000 fatalities from an attack on all operational SAC bases, assuming maximum utilization of existing civil defense facilities. This level is some two orders of magnitude less than the apocalyptic numbers that have been released in the past to show the inconceivability of strategic nuclear warfare. This report, however, generated substantial con-troversy, and many of the conclusions were later revised somewhat according to different ana-lytical assumptions. See *Analysis of Effects of Limited Nuclear War.* Prepared for the Subcom-mittee on Arms Control, International Organization, and Security Agreements, Committee on Foreign Relations, U.S. Senate. (Washington, D.C.: U.S. Government Printing Office, 1975.)

While it may be too much to expect a rigorous resolution of this controversy, one can examine the subject on a relative basis. Since the laws of physics, compared with the vicissitudes of warfare and the rhetoric of nuclear politics, do represent factual data, two kinds of comparisons might be made in the process of resolving the discrimination issue: (1) the collateral damage-producing effects from large-yield fission warheads—signifying the "Hiroshima image" of nuclear warfare —with those much lower yield and/or more advanced, refined warheads; and (2) the possible collateral damage-producing effects from conventional weapons associated with large-scale ground warfare with those from advanced, refined nuclear warheads.

To assess rigorously and fully the collateral damage differences between large- and small-yield fission warheads and advanced refined warheads calls for an analysis of such scope and detail that it is beyond this essay. However, since the difference is very large, it can be treated adequately, without such rigor, in a limited fashion.

To illustrate the point, we shall place the enquiry in a nuclear battlefield arena where (in view of our understanding of Soviet tactics) the primary problem involves defense against a massive attack by enemy armored units. In this respect, we might compare these advanced warhead possibilities with the large-yield fission warhead characteristic of much of current U.S. battlefield nuclear weapons.

As an example, we shall select the warhead in the Honest John rocket, which is reported to have a yield in the Hiroshima-bomb range, and compare it with a hypothesized enhanced radiation warhead (popularly known as the neutron bomb), which derives its effectiveness from nuclear fusion processes that release the bulk of their energy (about 80 percent) in the form of prompt nuclear radiation.[30]* In effect, this is comparing a 15-kiloton fission warhead with a 1-kiloton enhanced radiation warhead.

For both types of warheads, it is more effective to attack personnel —in the open or in armored vehicles—by making use of the prompt nuclear radiation effects than by trying to destroy the armored vehicles (tanks, armored personnel carriers) through blast effects. For fission warheads, the prompt radiation is emitted in the form of energetic neutrons and gamma rays; for enhanced radiation warheads, this radia-

*As contrasted with delayed nuclear radiation, which is normally associated with the radioactive decay of the products of nuclear fission.

tion consists of much more highly energetic neutrons. Because the enhanced radiation warhead fusion processes produce several times the amount of prompt radiation produced by the fission process and, moreover, produce substantially more penetrating radiation, the so-called "radiation kill" effectiveness of this warhead is equivalent to that of a much larger yield fission warhead. Hence, the same military results can be achieved through much lower yield weapons, thereby reducing troop safety hazards and potentially reducing collateral damage quite substantially.

In an effort to understand the nature and effectiveness of prompt nuclear radiation as a battlefield antipersonnel weapon, the Department of Defense has sponsored research in this area for many years. Based upon this research (as well as other knowledge of the biological effects of radiation, including that derived from the evaluation of a number of accidents involving humans) an advanced, if not thorough, understanding of the potential effects of prompt radiation on combat personnel has evolved. The most recent assessment and formulation of battlefield radiation casualty criteria was made by the U.S. Army and approved by the Joint Chiefs of Staff in 1975. Prompt radiation effects on the human body were described in terms of three major syndromes:

> *Central Nervous System (CNS) Syndrome: The threshold dose is about 2000 rads.* CNS symptoms are usually visible within minutes of exposure, and, depending upon the dose, the prodromal symptoms may or may not be observed. Typical CNS symptoms range from apathy and drowsiness to convulsions and collapse. The latter two are characteristic of doses above 5000 rads and lead to death within two days.*
>
> *Gastrointestinal (GI) Syndrome: The threshold dose is approximately 500 rads. An initial period of radiation sickness which may last as long as three days normally precedes the appearance of the GI syndrome symptoms which are usually first seen from three to five days following exposure. Typical symptoms progress from loss of appetite and vomiting to severe diarrhea, high fever and coma. Doses over 1000 rads lead to GI syndrome-related deaths and usually occur within two weeks.*
>
> *Hematopoietic Syndrome: The threshold dose is about 100 rads. In this case, the blood-forming organs have been damaged, principally the red bone marrow. The prodromal phase of radiation sickness runs its course, normally ending on the third day. There is then a so-called latent period during which no symptoms of radiation sickness are evidenced. The he-*

---

*The rad is a unit of absorbed radiation roughly equivalent to a roentgen, which is commonly used in measurements describing human biological responses to radiation exposure.

matopoietic syndrome symptoms are usually first seen two to three weeks after the exposure. Typical symptoms are chills and fever, headaches and easy fatigability which is the rapid exhaustion following exertions. Few deaths are expected due to the hemapoietic syndrome for doses below 200 rads. With higher doses, the more severe symptoms are evidenced such as purpura, which is bleeding under the skin resulting in patches of purplish discolorations, and bleeding from the gums. Deaths from this syndrome occur from three weeks to two months following irradiation.

For a nuclear battlefield situation, for example one involving a massive armored attack on Western Europe by Soviet/Pact forces, the first two syndromes (CNS and GI) are of particular significance. The question in terms of the effectiveness of their impact in stopping or disrupting such an attack has to do with human response over time. Times of significance for military combat purposes may run from minutes to hours depending upon the situation, and the tasks and location of the affected personnel. For correlating levels of radiation exposure and response times, the current Army radiation casualty guidelines are based upon the following distinctions:

Immediate Permanent Incapacitation (IP): 18,000-rad band (19,000 to 17,000 rads)—Personnel will become incapacitated within five minutes of exposure and for any task will remain incapacitated until death. Death will occur within one day.

8000-rad band (9000 to 7000 rads)—Personnel will become incapacitated within five minutes of exposure and for physically demanding tasks will remain incapacitated until death. Death will occur in one to two days.

Immediate Transient Incapacitation (IT): 3000-rad band (3500 to 2500 rads)—Personnel will become incapacitated within five minutes of exposure and will remain so for 30 to 45 minutes. Personnel will then recover but will be functionally impaired until death. Death will occur in four to six days.

Latent Lethality (LL): 650-rad band (800 to 500 rads)—Personnel will become functionally impaired within two hours of exposure. Personnel may respond to medical treatment and survive this dose; however, the majority of exposed personnel will remain functionally impaired until death in several weeks.[31]

Returning now to the comparison of a 15-kiloton fission warhead and a 1-kiloton enhanced radiation warhead, and using the Immediate Permanent Incapacitation for physically demanding tasks, defined above, the scale of blast and prompt radiation effects from these two warheads is shown in Table 1.

Table 1

Weapon	Tank Crew Incapacitation (radiation)	Tank Destruction (blast)	Urban Destruction (blast)	Radius of Damage in Meters Civilian Casualties (blast and radiation)
Enhanced Radiation— 1 Kiloton	700	150	500	1,000
Fission— 15 Kilotons	700	350	1,200	1,200

It is clear from this data that:

1. The dominant kill mechanism against armored units is that of crew incapacitation from prompt nuclear radiation. (This dominance is emphasized in some Soviet military literature on antitank warfare.)[32] For this kill mechanism, a kiloton enhanced-radiation warhead has about the same range of effectiveness as a 15-kiloton fission warhead (about the Hiroshima yield).
2. For the same military effectiveness (where attacks against armored units are being made), the fission warhead produces urban destruction from blast at a range some 70 percent larger than the range of military effects.
3. For the same level of military effectiveness, the fission warhead produces civilian casualties at a range of roughly 70 percent greater than the range of military effects; whereas for the enhanced radiation warhead, the casualties range is approximately 40 percent greater if civilians take *no* protective measures, and it can be substantially below the military range (almost to the point of disappearing) if civilians take elementary defense measures (e.g., the relatively simple expedient of providing additional shielding such as dirt or sand bags to that normally afforded by residential basements).

It is to be noted, therefore, that the substitution of an enhanced radiation warhead for a much larger yield fission warhead provides the same military effectiveness against units in the field, but without the radii of collateral damage extending well beyond the radii of military effects. As a consequence, where enemy units are operating near urban areas, the enhanced radiation warheads can provide discriminate attack possibilities, in contrast to the substantial collateral damage that may otherwise result from the use of higher-yield fission warheads.*

A familiar specter in conventional warfare is the systematic destruction, using high explosives, of contested urban areas. The list of European cities in World War II that were subjected to massive levels of damage and destruction is imposing; and should Western Europe become a conventional battleground once again, it is quite possible that a repetition of the World War II experience would occur.

The basic reason for extensive physical devastation in conventional urban warfare is that urban structure provides substantial protection against conventional weapon effects. In order to dislodge troops from defensive positions in urban areas, it frequently becomes necessary to attack at highly destructive levels.

On the other hand, whereas urban structure is usually sufficient to attenuate bullets and shell fragments substantially, it has but little effect on the transmission of neutrons and gamma rays. In this respect, were enhanced radiation weapons to be used against a city significantly occupied by enemy forces, by bursting the weapons at high altitude— in order to keep intense blast pressures from the surface—it becomes possible to produce wide-scale radiation-induced enemy casualties without attendant serious structural damage.

This is in sharp contrast with the devastation that would result (in attempts to attack and dislodge troops from urban areas) from large-yield fission weapons (e.g., Hiroshima-sized) or from massive conventional assaults, such as those that largely destroyed Berlin in World War II and Seoul during the Korean War.

As for the technical possibilities for enhanced radiation warheads, they were apparently recognized and (short of pure fusion anyway) tested successfully by the AEC more than a dozen years ago. A 1960 *Foreign Affairs* article by a Princeton physicist discussed these weapons in glowing terms.[33] And, in 1963, the merits of a pure-fusion

---

*Official recognition of this potential is found in Schlesinger's Nunn amendment report: "Further reductions in collateral damage can be made by improvements in weapon systems (e.g., reduced yields, special warhead effects such as enhanced radiation . . .)" (Department of Defense, *Theater Nuclear Force Posture in Europe,* p. 21.)

enhanced-radiation warhead compared with one having a fission trigger became the subject of open debate between Adrian Fisher, deputy director of the Arms Control and Disarmament Agency, and Senator Thomas Dodd. Fisher wrote:

> With respect to the pure fusion bomb, it should be pointed out that the development of such a weapon is by no means certain. However, as you know, we have already made significant advances in the direction of tactical weapons with a smaller fission as compared with fusion component. There is, therefore, a real question as to the utility of a pure fusion bomb over weapons already available. . . . Frankly, I don't think a possible reaction to the tactical use of nuclear weapons by us would be very much different whether it were a matter of our developing and using fusion weapons or an enhanced radiation weapon of a type now available.[34]

Beyond these early indications of the technological potential of such weapons, it was reported in 1967 that research on enhanced radiation weapons was continuing. In a press interview, the AEC was queried and answered as follows:

> Q. What progress is being made on "advanced concepts" of nuclear arms —such as the so-called neutron bomb?
> A. The AEC is conducting research on enhanced radiation weapons— neutron bombs. Such a device would be very "clean."[35]

It was not, however, until June 1977 that it became publicly known (through a widely publicized Washington *Post* report based upon congressional testimony in March) that an enhanced radiation warhead had been developed and was to be incorporated in the Army's Lance missile. Testifying for the Energy Research & Development Agency (ERDA), the Assistant Administrator for National Security, Lt. General Alfred D. Starbird (USA, Ret.), told a House Committee that the W70-3 ER warhead was about to enter production:

> We will actually start in two years delivering one of these weapons—it is one for the Lance missile.
> You reduce the blast effect and get the kill radius you want through enhanced radiation.[36]

Shortly thereafter, on June 24, the *Post* reported that a program to develop an enhanced radiation warhead for the Army's 8-inch howitzer had been underway, and was nearly complete, and that research funds had been sought to develop this capability for the 155-millimeter howitzer as well.

As a result of these revelations, and the prominence given them by the media, an intense national debate arose over the desirability of producing such weapons. Opponents, while generally not denying that use of such weapons could greatly reduce undesirable collateral damage, based their arguments principally on that very phenomenon, asserting that such "more usable" nuclear weapons would lower the nuclear threshold and make nuclear war more likely. Others capitalized on the description of the weapon as an anti-personnel weapon, carrying reduced blast damage to equipment and buildings, to portray it dramatically as a "people-killer" and "property-preserver." To both, the advanced discriminative effects promised by ER were not regarded as attractive. Proponents argued that a more discriminating weapon would actually strengthen deterrence of an enemy attack, by making their use on allied territory more credible, while at the same time reducing damage to the friendly territory that was to be defended should deterrence fail. This case was made strongly by supporters such as Senator Sam Nunn, and was apparently accepted fully by President Carter who sent the following letter to Senator Stennis urging appropriation of the funds requested for the ER weapon:

> [*The White House, Washington, dated July 11, 1977*]
>
> *To Senator John Stennis*
>
> *In reply to your July 6, 1977 letter, let me bring you up to date on my thinking with regard to the enhanced radiation (ER) weapons.*
>
> *I have requested that the Department of Defense provide me a study of such weaponry by August 15, 1977; it will be accompanied by an Arms Control Impact Statement (ACIS). I intend to make a final production decision shortly after receiving these two documents. If the production decision is an affirmative one, I will send the Congress the ACIS at the time my decision is announced.*
>
> *In the interim, the Department of Defense has prepared for me an initial assessment of these weapons. It is my present view that the enhanced radiation weapon contained in the ERDA budget is in this Nation's security interest. I therefore urge Congress to approve the current funding request.*
>
> *We are not talking about some new kind of weapon, but of the modernization of nuclear weapons. In the absence of satisfactory agreements to*

reduce nuclear weapons we must retain and modernize our theater nuclear capabilities, especially in support of NATO's deterrent strategy of response. Tactical nuclear weapons, including those for battlefield use, have strongly contributed to deterrence of conflict in Europe. I believe we must retain the option they provide and modernize it. These weapons are not strategic and have no relationship to SALT.

It must be recognized that NATO is a defensive alliance which might have to fight on its own territory. An aggressor should be faced with uncertainty as to whether NATO would use nuclear weapons against its forward echelons. For these purposes, the capability for discreet application of force—which the ER weapons may provide—present (at least in this sense) an attractive option. Whether or not the weapons have significant destabilizing aspects requires and will receive study in the ACIS.

The ER weapons, then, would be designed to enhance deterrence, but if deterrence fails to satisfy dual criteria:

—First, to enhance NATO's capability to inflict significant military damage on the aggressor.

—Second, to minimize damage and casualties to individuals not in the immediate target area, including friendly troops and civilians.

The decision to use nuclear weapons of any kind, including ER weapons, would remain in my hands, not in the hands of local theater commanders. A decision to cross the nuclear threshold would be the most agonizing decision to be made by any President. I can assure you that these weapons would not make that decision any easier. But by enhancing deterrence, they could make it less likely that I would have to face such a decision.

You had asked about the attitude of our NATO Allies with respect to ER weapons. Detailed information and our rationale for development of the warheads were provided to the NATO Nuclear Planning Group (NPG) Ministers of Defense in January 1976. Technical information was also provided to the NPG permanent representatives in the fall of 1976. The NATO authorities have supported the ER weapons program as being necessary to improve the effectiveness of NATO's theater nuclear force posture.

I hope the above information will prove useful to you in your upcoming debates on these weapons.

Sincerely [signed], Jimmy Carter [to] The Honorable John C. Stennis, United States Senate, Washington, D.C. 20510

Returning to the previously noted differences of opinion on possibilities for discriminate tactical nuclear warfare (McNamara versus Dulles), it would appear that the exploitation of fusion technology could provide a class of battlefield weapons conforming to the potential described by Secretary of State Dulles in 1957.

Specifically, enhanced radiation warheads offer possibilities for reducing collateral damage radii to levels well within the range of military effects—in sharp contrast to large-yield fission warheads, the collateral effects of which reach substantially beyond the military effects.

The specific enhanced radiation-fission warhead comparison given above assumed a required radius of military effectiveness, which called for a fission yield of 15 kilotons. Whereas this requirement may indeed be legitimate, there may be some number of enemy troop dispositions that can be covered sufficiently with much smaller lethal radii. For such cases, the use of subkiloton fission warheads may suffice to provide adequate target coverage but without serious levels of attendant collateral damage.

What fraction of the targets might call for subkiloton fission warheads cannot be predicted. However, one thing to be considered is that Soviet armored commanders, anticipating nuclear attacks against their units, may order maximum dispersal of vehicles to minimize the effectiveness of such attacks.

> It is impossible to determine the width of a front of attack purely arithmetically, without consideration of the concrete conditions of the situation. The size of the front of attack depends not only on the composition of friendly forces, the nature of the defense, and density of enemy men and material, but also on other factors, and above all, on the use of nuclear weapons [emphasis added]. . . . It is impossible to win a battle just by dispersal alone. A reasonable compromise must be found here between the requirements for troop protection and the need for successful accomplishment of the combat mission.[37]

How far the Soviet commander might go in dispersing his force to reduce vulnerability to nuclear attack is not certain. However, such measures could readily increase unit dimensions to levels where large-yield, highly destructive fission warheads are required to provide adequate target coverage. In this event, for the reasons given above, enhanced radiation warheads could provide the coverage, but without excessive collateral damage resulting.

As to classes of more or less hard physical targets that might be considered for nuclear attack, the potential for discriminate attack is more a function of weapon-delivery accuracy than of warhead technology. In this respect, advanced guidance systems now under development promise to provide delivery errors sufficiently small to allow effective nuclear attack of some targets with yields in the subkiloton range. At such low levels of yield, and for attack against such physical targets as bridges and hardened command posts, the collateral damage potential may not represent a sufficient problem to make a strong case for advanced warhead technology beyond that now existing for small and fairly efficient fission warheads.

However, were one to make a case based on warhead technology, the potential exists for a class of very low yield, "clean," suppressed radiation warheads that produce no significant nuclear radiation effects, prompt or delayed. In effect, such warheads would represent a massive high-explosive charge, but in a far smaller and lighter package.

Soviet Warhead Technology

> *Rather than building large numbers of shortrange, low-yield systems . . . the Soviets have emphasized higher-yield, mobile tactical missiles, primarily useful for terrain or blanketing fires. Indeed, the Soviet force structure raises serious doubts about their* capability *to fight a limited tactical nuclear war, much less one in which collateral damage and civilian casualties are to be kept to low levels. (Alain C. Enthoven and K. Wayne Smith)*
>
> *We have little certain knowledge of the Soviet warhead designs, of their vulnerability, or of Soviet testing or development philosophy. . . . We do not know what the Soviets have accomplished in their test program since 1963, but unless their program was a very sterile one, the Soviets would almost certainly be in a far more favorable position to upgrade their future stockpile with even more effective tactical and strategic systems. (Carl Walske)*
>
> *Through the efforts of scientists, designers, engineers, workers, and military specialists, nuclear warheads of various power levels . . . have been created.*[38] *(Marshal K. Kazakov)*

Here, we have conflicting statements regarding the Soviet nuclear stockpile, one expressing apparently certain knowledge of Soviet emphasis on high-yield warheads, another avowing uncertainty in U.S. knowledge, and a Soviet statement indicating a coordinated technical-military effort to create a range of required warhead yields. Since one must regard the statement by Dr. Walske (then Assistant to the Secretary of Defense for Atomic Energy), in official congressional testimony as representing the official U.S. Defense Department position, it would appear that the Enthoven-Smith assessment is based more on projecting

Soviet warhead requirements by their own criteria (or preferences for the sake of argumentation) than on concrete knowledge. This seems even more so since Walske's statement, given in 1971, has been supported more recently by those in good positions to know our state of knowledge. As two examples: In a report to the Congress in 1973, then chairman of the Joint Chiefs of Staff, Admiral Thomas H. Moorer, stated:

> *It is difficult to draw precise conclusions as to the relative balance between the U.S. and the USSR in theater nuclear weapons. This is so because of the uncertainties inherent in estimating Soviet nuclear weapons inventories, as well as the problems involved in evaluating Soviet nuclear weapons technology, now that all testing is conducted underground.*[39]

And in a statement in 1976, ERDA's deputy assistant administrator for national security, Major General Edward Giller (USAF, Retired) noted:

> *Early Soviet tactical nuclear systems were apparently high yield weapons. We are much less certain about the systems they have introduced in recent years. Those who argue that U.S. introduction of low collateral damage tactical nuclear weapons is meaningless as long as the Soviets maintain high yields ignore the possibility that the Soviets have already moved toward lower yield systems or will do so in response to the U.S. initiative.*[40]

Since many argue that the composition of the Soviet stockpile relates importantly to NATO tactical nuclear requirements and to the political credibility of the U.S. tactical nuclear warheads, it is important to determine whether the exclusive high-yield assessment reflects the probable nature of the Soviet stockpile or whether a different interpretation seems equally or more plausible. As Congressman Craig Hosmer, then a long-time member of the Joint Committee on Atomic Energy, noted pointedly:

> *If, indeed, the Soviets have been busy perfecting a family of clean, discriminate, tactical nuclear weapons and the time should ever come when they decide to use them against us and our allies, a time will come when the devastation and contamination from tactical nuclear war will come from our stockpile.*[41]

While sufficient hard data on Soviet nuclear warheads has been lacking since the Partial Test Ban Treaty went into effect in 1963, there was ample evidence before then that the Soviets had achieved technical competence in thermonuclear (fusion) designs, although for high yields, and the ability to eventually produce a range of warhead yields and types. (Whether they tested or developed low-yield fusion devices during this period is an open question, since the U.S. capability to analyze test debris—particularly for low-yield tests—was of questionable effectiveness, even at that time.) *

That the Soviets have long been familiar with the basic nature of enhanced radiation weapons is well established by a 1958 paper on pure fusion explosive research (which was conducted as early as 1952) delivered by Soviet physicist L. A. Artsimovich. An extract from this paper contained the following remarks:

> A pulsed thermonuclear reaction may also be possible under conditions when a high temperature is reached during the compression and implosion produced . . . by a charge of conventional explosives (such as TNT or something more powerful) surrounding a capsule of deuterium or a mixture of deuterium and tritium. Without going into details of the experiments, it should be mentioned that the conditions have been found under which the generations of neutrons both in the $D + T$ and the $D + D$ reactions is detected with absolute reliability and reproducibility. . . . In experiments conducted in 1952, it was possible to record both fast neutrons that passed through the charge without any great loss of energy as well as neutrons that were slowed down in the explosive.[42]

Apparently we do not fully know what has transpired in the Soviet Union's nuclear weapons development program during the ensuing nearly quarter century, and what their current technological level in this area may be. However, it would be both unwise and unreasonable to assume that they have so dramatically limited themselves in their flexible and effective weaponry. If the Soviets elected to pursue a program leading to the attainment of an enhanced radiation warhead of a fission-fusion type, or other tailored effects weapons, it would be imprudent to assume that they could not by now have stockpiled such

*To quote Hosmer again: "It should be understood that our knowledge of Soviet nuclear weapons is based far more upon speculation than upon cold, hard facts. Edward Teller has described our process of evaluation as akin to trying to determine a neighbor's cooking by means of sniffing the smoke from his kitchen. Evaluation of this kind must, of necessity, be highly narcissistic, in that we must guess the Soviet technology by assuming that it is essentially the same as ours. To put it mildly, such methods are bound to be highly inaccurate and subject to human interpretation." (Representative Craig Hosmer on March 21, 1963, *Congressional Record,* April 15, 1963, p. A-2306.)

weapons, considering that the United States had the option for such stockpiling more than twelve years ago.

Although firm evidence indicating established Soviet requirements for discriminate tactical nuclear weapons is lacking, some recent writings on battlefield nuclear use seem to show a disposition toward the use of prompt nuclear radiation as a primary kill-mechanism for the attack of armored units. (In contrast, the United States has, in the past, based its tactical nuclear warhead requirements on blast effects against troops and material.) In this regard, a recent Soviet book on antitank warfare contains the following observations:

> *The destructive effect of nuclear weapons on armored troops represents a tremendous increase over that of conventional weapons. Nuclear attacks can inflict enormous losses on man and machines. However, in performing the mission of destroying armored troops on the field of battle, it is expedient to destroy such a basic element as the tank crews in and outside the tanks. This makes it possible to deprive the enemy armored troops of their combat power with a greater economy of ammunition, in shorter periods, and with a high destructive probability.*
>
> *The point is that the effective radius of a nuclear explosion is one and a half to twice as great against a tank crew as it is against a tank (3–4 times as great in the case of low-yield explosions). Consequently, the effective zone of the same explosion is about 3–4 (9–16) times larger for crews than for the tanks.*[43]

To confirm the above-given ratios of "radiation kill" to "blast kill" radii, a tabulation of kill radii for fission weapons of different yields (compiled by the Soviet authors) is presented in Table 2.

Table 2

Yield (Kilotons)	Radius of Damage in Meters	
	Medium Tanks	Crews in Tanks
0.02	25	130
0.5	120	340
2.5	200	500
10	350	700
20	450	800
100–150	600	900
100–150	800–1,000	1,100–1,300
500	1,700	1,700

Table 2 brings out two key factors:

1. Even for yields at the (extremely destructive) 100-kiloton level, prompt radiation effects are the dominant kill-mechanism. Before blast becomes the prevailing effect, yields of hundreds of kilotons seem required.
2. Keeping in mind the much greater prompt radiation effectiveness of enhanced radiation weapons, as compared with fission weapons, it is plausible to conjecture that a Soviet preference for "radiation kill" would carry a preference for enhanced radiation weapons.

As brought out previously, a hypothesized enhanced-radiation warhead may have a prompt nuclear radiation effectiveness comparable to that of a fission warhead having a fifteenfold greater yield. On this basis, a one-kiloton enhanced-radiation warhead could be substituted for a fifteen-kiloton fission warhead to provide the terrain fire capability ascribed by Enthoven and Smith, but with a small fraction of the blast and even less of the radioactivity effects. As another alternative, two one-kiloton enhanced-radiation warheads could be substituted for one fission warhead having a yield of a few hundred kilotons, and the distinctions are correspondingly more dramatic.

Soviet tactical nuclear military literature stresses the necessity for offensive armored units to operate effectively in areas where nuclear bursts have taken place, even where they have producd extensive areas of devastation (e.g., tree blowdown and conflagration in forested areas) and radiological contamination. (The general assumption seems to be that these unwanted effects will arise from the enemy nuclear bursts.) At the same time, the requirements for limiting destructive effects through use of their own weapons is noted.* In this connection, considering the primary emphasis given by the Soviets to "blitzkrieg" armored operations, the characteristics of enhanced-radiation warheads, as well as a range of warhead yields at levels consistent with selective battlefield use, should be appealing—fully aside from Soviet views on civilian collateral damage.

---

*"Under the conditions prevailing in a city, employment of nuclear weapons is limited in as much as they entail extensive destruction, piled rubble, and regions which are almost impassable not only for the enemy but for friendly troops." (Major General A. K. Shokolovich, Colonel F. I. Konasov, and Colonel S. I. Tkach, *Action of a Motorized Rifle Battalion in a City* (Moscow, 1971), U.S. Army Translation No. K-1400, p. 6.)

Once again, it must be emphasized that the Soviet tactical nuclear stockpile is not of a quality fully known to the United States. However, to the extent that a punitive high-yield and indiscriminate Soviet stockpile remains a U.S. planning factor, it can be suggested that this assessment has reflected a *U.S.* indisposition toward discriminate tactical nuclear capabilities, and toward planning for a TNW battlefield, in spite of its lack of hard evidence. It is, in short, merely another example of "mirror-imaging" our own strategic concepts and preferences to the Soviets'. It also serves handily to buttress the case against our developing such weapons. As the argument goes: What good would it do for us when (if) they don't? However, the line of reasoning for which the Soviets have opted in order to retain a high-yield, indiscriminate, fission warhead tactical nuclear stockpile seems to lack the solid evidence to make it persuasive, much less presumptive. It fits neither the technology available to the Soviets, nor their interest in modern, flexible weapons, nor their strategic philosophy, which emphasizes a strong coupling of political and military objectives even for nuclear war.

In this regard, there have been strong indications from Soviet sources over the years that large-scale urban-industrial collateral damage, in the event of a war in Europe, was regarded not only as not desirable, but as something that might be avoided.* Contrary to much Western literature about the "uncontrollability" of damage in the event of nuclear war in Europe, the Soviet general staff—according to its professional journal, *Voyennaya Mysl'*—has dealt seriously with problems of selective targeting precisely to *preserve* assets in territory to be occupied, while at the same time destroying or neutralizing enemy military forces. Classic military principles of "economy of force" seem also to have been present in Soviet military thought:

> *Initial attention is given to the selection of those enemy targets against which nuclear means could best be used. Depending on the features of the strike targets, a selection is made of the nuclear weapon carriers . . . which could best and most rapidly execute the assigned mission with minimum expenditure of explosive power."* (MGEN V. Kruchinin, "Contemporary Strategic Theory on the Goals and Missions of Armed Conflict," Voyennaya Mysl', FPD 965, 20 July 1966, Issue 10, October 1963, p. 17.)

*This is made clear by research performed by Dr. Joseph Douglass, System Planning Corporation, on previously classified copies of the journal of the Soviet General Staff, *Voyennaya Mysl'* (*Military Thought*). Dr. Douglass's work, available in SPC reports, is soon to be published. The quotations are drawn from that work.

The political and strategic reasoning behind this is explicit:

> *The objective is not to turn the large economic and industrial regions into a heap of ruins . . . but to deliver strikes which will destroy strategic combat means, paralyze enemy military production, making it incapable of satisfying the priority needs of the front and rear areas and sharply reduce the enemy capability to conduct strikes. (Col. M. Shirokov, "Military Geography at the Present Stage," Voyennaya Mysl', No. 11, November 1966, Foreign Press Digest FPD 730/67, 27 July 1967, p. 59.)*

Consistently Clausewitzian in their approach to military matters, military power is used according to the political objectives of the CPSU:

> *Theses of Soviet military strategy primarily reflect the political strategy of the Communist Party of the Soviet Union. It is in the interests of political strategy that military strategy makes use of the achievements of scientific-technical progress which materialize in weapons of varying power. Some of these weapons are capable of doing considerable damage to a continent, others only to individual states. . . . Finally, still others lead to defeat of the enemy's armed forces without doing essential injury to the economy or populace of states whose aggressive rulers unleashed the war. Only political leadership can determine the scale and consistency of bringing to bear the most powerful means of destruction. (L.Gen G. Semenov and M.Gen V. Prokhorov, "Scientific-Technical Progress and Some Questions of Strategy," Voyennaya Mysl', No. 2, February 1969, FPD-060/69, 18 June 1969, p. 23.)*

Assertions of some Western writers, such as those quoted at the start of this section, that the ability to fight a limited nuclear war, "much less one in which collateral damage and civilian casualties are to be kept to low levels," is not in the Soviet force structure are clearly at odds with options made explicit by the Soviet general staff.

U.S. and USSR Tactical Nuclear Weapons Systems

> *But, however much the original initiative lay with us, the Soviet Union has shown the liveliest possible interest in the concept of theater nuclear warfare. As a consequence, it is now the Soviets who set the pace here, as they do in so many other respects.*
>
> *Soviet peripheral attack and theater nuclear forces are numerous, diversified, and of high quality.[44] (Secretary of Defense James Schlesinger)*
>
> *In terms of their combat properties, the missiles of our Ground Troops are not only not inferior to the foreign ones, but surpass them in a number of important indexes.[45] (Soviet Defense Minister A. A. Grechko)*

Although it has been about twenty years since the Soviet Union embarked upon its tactical nuclear buildup, there has been little attention to it publicly and little official concern expressed over it. Yet, as the above statements indicate, the Soviets have been striving to develop nuclear weapons with maximum theater war-fighting capabilities, and these capabilities, vis-à-vis those of the West, deserve closer and more critical attention than has been given them so far.

On the U.S. side, a major thrust of tactical nuclear developments has been in the direction of providing dual-capable systems, with a requirement to provide, in the same weapons, an effective conventional capability. As a consequence, U.S. "TNW" forces contain a relatively large family of weapons that are also part of conventional defense, with early nonnuclear roles assigned to them.

How wise is this criterion of a dual-capable system remains a matter of contention, as does the potential effectiveness or ineffectiveness of the system in war. Dual-capable systems are very seldom optimal for either a tactical nuclear or a conventional role, leaving aside planning and operational difficulties of changing systems from one to the other. Some weapons, such as the F-111 fighter-bomber and the Lance surface-to-surface missile, are of most dubious conventional utility.

On the Soviet side, the evidence to date suggests that primary attention has been paid to combined arms forces—employing nuclear and conventional weapons—but not in the context of dual-capable systems. Instead, the emphasis has been on designing nuclear and conventional weapons that can best complement each other in a nuclear-dominated environment. In this framework, the Soviets apparently assigned the primary nuclear role to highly mobile surface-to-surface rockets and ballistic missiles. As argued in 1971 by Soviet Defense Minister Grechko, "Nuclear missiles will be the decisive means of armed combat."[46]

That tactical aviation and artillery may have been regarded in the past primarily for nonnuclear aspects of combined operations has been hinted in Soviet military literature:

> The principle of the employment of nuclear weapons in combination with other means of destruction *follows from the fact that it is impossible to destroy all varied objectives on the battlefield with nuclear weapons alone. It is believed that nuclear weapons, as the main means of destruction, will be employed only for the destruction of the most important ob-*

jectives; all other targets are neutralized and destroyed by the artillery, aviation, and the fire of tanks and other weapons. In other words, nuclear weapons are deployed in combination with other means in accordance with the concept of battle.[47] *(Emphasis in original.)*

However, recent evidence indicates that aviation and other weapons are being given a major nuclear role.

Soviet tactical air forces have increasingly been given a strike capability and an extensive nuclear delivery capability, although the magnitude of the role they may play in tactical nuclear operations has not yet been made clear. Evidence that Soviet Frontal Aviation has been given significantly enhanced nuclear strike capabilities in recent years, however, points to a correspondingly enhanced role, complementing ground forces and rockets. (Pointing out that air bases, even when individual aircraft are heavily sheltered, are highly vulnerable to nuclear attack, some have postulated that Soviet air-delivered nuclear weapons may be used in concert with ballistic missiles in a surprise first-strike attack; others still feel that the bulk of the Soviet tactical air will be used for follow-up conventional operations and air-defense against NATO air strikes.)

In addition, there is increasing evidence that the Soviets have developed and are deploying nuclear warheads for 153-mm and 203-mm self-propelled artillery pieces. SACEUR General Alexander Haig recently discussed these possibilities, stating that while unambiguous evidence was still lacking, there are "lots of leads to suggest it's in the cooker."[48]

General Giller recently stated, "While we know comparatively little in the area of Soviet tactical nuclear weapons, the variety of their nuclear capable and tactical delivery systems is visibly increasing."[49]

Apparent differences in TNW design and employment philosophy between the United States and the USSR make it extremely difficult to make a net technical assessment of the two sides' capabilities. Such an assessment is heavily restricted by the "apples and oranges" quandary that envelops it. Moreover, nonweapons functions (such as vulnerability of the opposing target structure, initiative, timing, and purpose of use) and doctrine for nuclear operations critically affect such comparisons.

On the other hand, holding in abeyance the latter considerations, there are three areas where weapon performance comparisons become meaningful: mobility, range, and delivery performance. The first two relate critically to vulnerability, and the third to weapons effectiveness and discrimination.

Because of the high vulnerability of air bases to nuclear attack, plus the ambiguous nature of the nuclear role of Soviet aircraft, we shall make no attempt here to compare U.S.-NATO tactical aircraft with those of the USSR. Aircraft performance characteristics, for comparative purposes, are available in a number of open sources such as *Jane's All the World's Aircraft* and annual *Air Force Magazine* almanacs. In quantity, however, the Soviet-Pact nuclear-capable strike aircraft significantly outnumber those of the West in the Central European theater, and the Soviets have been introducing new models much faster than the United States has. In view of a lack of firm data on Soviet nuclear artillery capability, no comparative effort *can* be made in this area.* Nor, for the same reason, can an ADM assessment be made. And this narrows the comparison down to the surface-to-surface rockets and missiles that both sides have developed and deployed.

On the U.S. side, four classes of ballistic rockets and missiles now comprise this component of the tactical nuclear stockpile: Honest John, Sergeant, Pershing, and Lance.† (U.S. theater nuclear systems are listed in Table 3).

> *Honest John,* an unguided rocket, first entered the United States inventory in 1953. There have been no major modernization improvements since that time. It has a maximum range of 25 miles.
> *Sergeant,* a guided missile, became operational in 1962. There has been no significant modernization. It has a maximum range of 85 miles.
> *Pershing,* a guided missile, became operational in 1962. There are developments afoot to provide for a more accurate guid-

---

*In view of U.S.-NATO improvements in short-range antitank guided missiles (ATGMs)—such improvements having become a cause of major concern to Soviet planners—there would be a very logical requirement for Soviet nuclear artillery. Such a capability would provide the means to deal quickly, effectively, and safely (with respect to their own troops) with NATO front-line antitank defense concentrations, using low-yield warheads, and with other units as well. One low-yield nuclear round could provide almost instantaneously the equivalent firepower of a conventional artillery barrage involving tens of thousands of rounds delivered over many hours.
†Nike-Hercules, although designed for surface-air defense, might be regarded here in a surface-to-surface mode.

Table 3
U.S. Theater Nuclear Systems

System	Approximate Range (NM)	Approximate Yields	Stockpile Entry Date
Pershing	425–50	Intermediate kiloton-range, several yields	1962
Sergeant	85	Kiloton-range yields	1962
Lance*	75–80	Optional yields, sub-kiloton & kiloton	1974
Honest John	25	Low-kiloton	
8-inch howitzer*	10	Sub- to low-kiloton	1958
155-mm howitzer	10	Sub-kiloton	1964
F-104		Range of bomb yields from sub-kiloton to intermediate & high yields	1959–63
F-4			
FB-111			1968
Walleye ASM		Sub-kiloton	1972
Nike-Hercules (as SSM)	100+	Low-kiloton	1959
ADM		Sub-kiloton to a few kilotons	1962–65

*Depending on the President's decision, ER warheads developed for Lance and the 8-inch howitzer may be produced and deployed. These would be the first such advanced TNW warheads to be put into the deployed stockpile. As described in the FY 1977 Department of Defense report (p. 105), this artillery projectile "greatly reduces undesired collateral damage."

ance and, thus, a lower-yield, more discriminate capability. It has a range of 425–50 miles.

Lance, a guided missile, began to enter the force in 1974, but the technology is over a decade old. It has a range of about 75 miles.

On the Soviet side, three classes of weapons now exist—FROG, Scud, and Scaleboard; however, a new, follow-on Scud and/or a mobile missile with a range between Scud and Scaleboard have been suggested:*

*The SS-14, Scamp, a mobile medium-range missile of some 1500 nm range, and the more recently developed SS-20, a mobile intermediate-range ballistic missile, are not included here, nor are the fixed medium- and intermediate-range ballistic missiles, since all are deployed—so far—within the Soviet Union. However, it now appears that the SS-20 is in steady production, and, if so, its deployment for theater purposes must be assumed.

FROG (Free Rocket Over Ground), an unguided rocket, first entered the Soviet inventory in 1957. However, since that time, there have been a series of model improvements; the latest version, known as FROG 7, was introduced in 1956. FROG 7 has a range up to 45 miles—about three times that of FROG 1.

Scud, a guided missile, first became operational in 1959. However, a model improvement, the Scud B, was introduced in 1965. It essentially doubled the missile's range, to about 150 miles, and there are clear indications of a newer model, Scud C.

Scaleboard (SS-12), a guided missile, entered the force in 1969. It has a range up to 500 miles and, apparently, good accuracy.[50]

Comparing the U.S. and Soviet rockets and missiles, two observations can be made: (1) The Soviet systems are, on an average, of considerably more recent vintage than those of the United States; and (2) The Soviet weapons have greater ranges and greater range versatility than do U.S. systems, particularly if the SS-20 is included. They are also apparently deployed in larger numbers.

Whereas it is not possible to translate these age and range disparities into specific military asymmetrics—as related to the conduct and outcome of a tactical nuclear conflict—nevertheless, they suggest a qualitative advantage on the side of the Soviets, in terms of whose rocket and missile units are more capable of striking targets on the other side.

Some have referred to NATO's alleged advantage in small-yield battlefield warheads, primarily on the basis of the U.S. nuclear artillery capability. For, barring Soviet terminal guidance systems at present, the accuracy of artillery is substantially better than that of unguided rockets and short-range mobile missiles, thereby permitting the effective delivery of small-yield warheads. Moreover, there are advantages from the greater proliferation of artillery and its use against close targets of opportunity. Aside from the obvious virtue of reducing levels of civilian collateral damage, the employment of small-yield warheads would allow a greater flexibility of operations in view of the increased safety to front-line troops.

However, this seeming advantage of U.S. artillery over Soviet rockets may be partly offset by the longer range of some missiles and must be evaluated in terms of how the Soviets regard the use of their nuclear weapons and what criteria they use to define the destruction of enemy battlefield targets. In this respect, it would appear that the U.S. advantage due to its artillery has been alleged on the basis that Soviet target-damage criteria have mirrored those that have long been adopted by the United States—namely, the requirement physically to damage or destroy enemy materiel.[51] (Materiel targets are tougher to destroy by blast than are personnel by prompt nuclear radiation; to achieve a given radius of effectiveness, a much lower yield can be selected if radiation is the selected target-kill mechanism; see table 1.) Were this projection to the Soviet warhead requirement process true, the assignment of large-yield warheads to compensate for the allegedly poorer accuracy of the rockets would, indeed, seem reasonable. However, if Soviet requirements were based on "radiation kill," it is not at all clear that this assignment can validly be made. (It is also not clear that the accuracy of the newer Soviet short-range guided missiles is so poor. This is an area where our ability to assess is quite poor; consequently, it would be most difficult—and imprudent—to maintain expectations of ever-poor accuracies, especially in view of the dramatic gains in accuracy of the Soviet ICBMs and IRBMs.)

If, indeed, the Soviets were to have based their warhead requirement process on "radiation kill" criteria and, in this framework, stockpiled enhanced radiation warheads, then the radius of effectiveness of low-yield enhanced radiation warheads could be entirely compatible with the magnitude of the delivery error. Moreover, the level of endangerment to their own troops would be substantially less than the value associated with a much larger yield based on a "blast kill" requirement; it could, in fact, not be substantially different from that associated with a low-yield artillery shell.

In summary, regarding the capabilities of U.S. and Soviet tactical nuclear delivery systems, there do not seem to be well-substantiated reasons for accepting the long-held claims on the U.S. side that the United States continues to maintain tactical nuclear superiority, based quirement; it could, in fact, not be substantially different from that upon alleged technology and hardware advantages, which would offset Soviet numerical advantages.* To the contrary, the Soviet propensity for model improvement and greater weapons innovation, as well as the significantly greater role of tactical nuclear operations in Soviet doctrine and training, and their massive deployments in Eastern Europe—

increasingly oriented to attack-without-warning capability—indicate a substantial potential advantage on their side. Since weapons comparisons cannot themselves be used to gauge relative combat effectiveness, the question of relative capabilities cannot be approached without examining doctrine and strategy.

Implications of a Comprehensive Test Ban Treaty for TNW Development

Immediately after assuming office, the Carter Administration vigorously renewed American efforts to achieve a comprehensive test ban treaty with the Soviet Union. Necessarily, the issue of verifying tests (low-yield) pertinent to TNW development arises, since—whatever level of seismic magnitude is argued for detection and identification of underground nuclear tests—there are tests that clearly cannot be identified by national technical means of verification. Any "comprehensive" test ban, in that sense, is of necessity a "threshold" test ban, applicable only to tests detectable above that threshold. Such a test ban would then provide a closed society such as the USSR with a one-sided opportunity to continue testing clandestinely, at least at low yields, and thereby develop a family of advanced TNW warheads.

There are many possibilities for unilateral advantages in nuclear technology to be gained from clandestine testing below the detection threshold, many of which are outside the subject of this monograph. In TNW technology, however, there should be concern about a situation where the United States scrupulously observed a test ban and the Soviet Union did not. In time, the USSR—virtually without fear of detection—could develop a family of low-yield, discriminate warheads whose use would not only provide far more effective battlefield employment but would also result in levels of collateral damage far less than those widely ascribed to local or theater nuclear war. The asymmetry of such capabilities would pose very serious political and military problems for the United States and NATO. The use of such weapons

---

[*] "The Soviets, in turn, evince extreme quantitative superiority in Central Europe, where their surface-to-surface missiles outnumber ours by about 10:1 and their 700 nuclear capable aircraft by something like two-to-one." (Library of Congress, *United States/Soviet Military Balance*, prepared for the Senate Committee on Armed Services [Washington, D.C.: Government Printing Office, 1976], p. 5.) In addition, SACEUR General Haig, in a recent statement, warned that Soviet forces in Eastern Europe are increasing in numbers, becoming more offensive in capability, and improving their capability to attack without reinforcements. [*Soviet Aerospace* 17, no. 11 (November 15, 1976), p. 79.]

would be highly credible, while collateral damage would be largely tied to any employment of U.S. weapons. The United States, having foreclosed this discriminate option through a cessation of testing, would face even more severe and one-sided political-military constraints on TNW employment than it does now.

In addition, it should be recalled that, to a very appreciable degree, the U.S. strategy of extending deterrence to allies through escalatory threats has been premised on the expectation that any Soviet theater nuclear use would be so destructive and escalatory, in itself, that further escalation by the West, including strategic strikes on the USSR, would be so likely as to be a highly credible deterrent threat to such Soviet use in the first place. That would not equally be the case for a very discriminate Soviet capability, the use of which would not result in widespread or large-scale collateral damage. Were the Soviets to have that capability, and the West not, the premises of Western deterrence strategy would be badly shaken, and the security ties of the alliance loosened.

Tactical Nuclear Military Capabilities

There are three issues relevant to tactical nuclear military capabilities that bear on the problem of net assessment: (1) the doctrine held by each side and each side's strategy for employment; (2) the planning assumptions held by each side as to the other's doctrine and strategy for use; and (3) the force posture of each side's deployment. In each of these areas, there are marked dissimilarities between the two sides.

Doctrine and Strategy

> While it is essential to theorize about the nature of tactical nuclear warfare, we must acknowledge that, as a practical matter, the initiation of a nuclear engagement would involve many uncertainties. Acceptable boundaries on such a conflict would be extremely difficult to establish. A nuclear engagement in the theater could well produce much higher military and civilian casualties and more widespread collateral damage than its non-nuclear counterpart. . . . What is more, it is not clear under what conditions the United States and its allies would possess a comparative military advantage in a tactical nuclear exchange. (James R. Schlesinger)

> The ground troops have gained new combat qualities. Their fire and striking power and their mobility have risen significantly and, as a result

of this, the ground troops have acquired even greater independence in carrying out combat missions in a war.

. . . In coordinating with the other types of Armed Forces and independently, they are capable of carrying out missions to defeat the enemy in the ground theaters of military actions. For this, the ground troops have operational and tactical missile units, air defense units, motorized rifle and tank combined units, various types of artillery, as well as special troops such as engineering, signal, and others.

The operational and tactical missile units comprise the basis for the firepower of the ground troops. This is a qualitatively new branch of arms which is the basic means for employing nuclear weapons in combat and operations. (A. A. Grechko)

The breakthrough of a prepared defense will be accomplished not by "gnawing through" as happened in the last war but by the launching of nuclear strikes and overcoming it by "fast movements" of tank and motorized rifle troops.[52] (Army General S. M. Shtemenko)

These views on the utility of tactical nuclear weapons are not only highly disparate, but they also raise questions as to whether the role of tactical nuclear weapons in NATO's overall doctrine is at all realistically related to the Soviets' doctrine for their ground forces.

On the U.S.-NATO side, the employment of tactical nuclear weapons is generally treated as far more theoretical than practical; as involving serious risks and uncertainties rather than representing a means to the achievement of military objectives; as an escalatory threat rather than a means of territorial defense; and as a dubious method for attaining a military advantage over a nuclear opponent who also will employ these weapons.

On the Soviet side, such employment seems to be regarded in a very positive and tangible way, as the primary means of firepower, and as a basis for defeating the enemy.

Yet NATO's doctrine places essential emphasis on conventional defense against a presumed nonnuclear attack. In effect, it is based on the premise that, faced with the moment of truth, the Soviets would elect to mobilize, mount, and sustain a conventional attack for a protracted period. Indeed, until stalemate! This evokes some wonderment as to whether the U.S.-NATO doctrine has been founded on *any* realistic assessment of Soviet thinking.

True, short of the issue being resolved by the advent of actual conflict, it is not possible to reach a definitive conclusion. The political nature of conflict may involve intangible considerations that would modify prevailing doctrine at the time of military conflict. However, on the NATO side, since prevailing doctrine and planning factors determine the peacetime defensive posture, and since a strategy based upon misperception of the enemy may result in military disaster, it is important to examine as best as possible the doctrine and strategy of both sides toward assessing credibility on the NATO side.

The U.S.-NATO Side

At the time U.S. TNW were first introduced into NATO a strategy emphasizing their use was positive and unequivocal; as then Deputy SACEUR Field Marshal Montgomery proclaimed:

> *I want to make it absolutely clear that we at Supreme Headquarters Allied Powers Europe are basing all our operational planning on using atomic and thermonuclear weapons in our defense. With us, it is no longer "they may be possibly used." It is very definitely, "they will be used if we are attacked."*[53]

Beginning in 1961, however, U.S. policy regarding TNW shifted drastically in the direction of nonuse. In moving toward a conventional emphasis policy, the United States, as President Kennedy put it, was seeking "a wider choice than humiliation or allout nuclear action." Implied here, as became progressively clear, was a fundamental belief in the disutility, and even essential hopelessness, of using tactical nuclear weapons in limited conflicts. As Kennedy put it, "Inevitably the use of small nuclear armaments will lead to larger and larger nuclear armaments on both sides, until the worldwide holocaust has begun."[54]

Subsequently, the attitude of U.S. and Allied NATO policymakers shifted to one of avoiding their use, with a consistency of view that saw Richard Nixon, upon becoming president, depart dramatically from the Eisenhower views to endorse those expressed by Kennedy:

> *Sole reliance upon early resort to nuclear weapons . . . would leave us no option between capitulation and risking all-out mutual destruction. Twenty years ago, ironically, when our conventional forces returned to Europe in strength, the U.S. enjoyed a nuclear monopoly and had perhaps*

less military need of a massive conventional presence. Today, when we no longer have this unilateral nuclear advantage, a NATO conventional option is needed as never before.[55]

At present, given the framework of the above remarks, the United States and NATO are lacking in doctrine, strategy, and forces for the employment of tactical nuclear weapons. This lack is buttressed by a long-held American belief (not universally concurred in by NATO allies) that the Soviet Union shares the West's apprehensions over the unpredictable consequences and highly dangerous risks from nuclear weapons use.

Somewhat ironically, given both the ingrained Western aversion to nuclear use (in contrast to the attitude of the Soviets) and the changed strategic nuclear balance, this belief has helped produce a strategy of threatened nuclear escalation that holds that the Soviets would not only begin war nonnuclearly but would back down in the face of Western resort to nuclear weapons. The following exchange took place between then SACEUR General Goodpaster and Senator Symington:

> *Sen. Symington: If we replied to a Soviet conventional attack by using tactical nuclear weapons, have you any doubt that they would immediately start using nuclear weapons, themselves?*
>
> *Gen. Goodpaster: I don't concede at all that they would. They might. But they would have to ask themselves the question that I referred to earlier and that is, what is there west of the Iron Curtain that would justify entering into a process of escalation that could involve an attack on their own homeland?*
>
> *Sen. Symington: Certainly they might. Is it your opinion that they probably would not?*
>
> *Gen. Goodpaster: My opinion is, and this is, of course, completely speculative—*
>
> *Sen. Symington: It is very important, though.*
>
> *Gen. Goodpaster: Yes, indeed.*
>
> *Sen. Symington: It couldn't be more so.*
>
> *Gen. Goodpaster: In the context that we are talking about, a large-scale non-nuclear attack against Western Europe, if we were to apply in a controlled way limited numbers of nuclear weapons sufficient simply to stop the attack and impose costs and losses on their attack echelons, my own feeling is that the probabilities would be much less than even that they would immediately carry that to all-out nuclear exchange involving their own homeland.*
>
> *Sen. Symington: In other words, your testimony before this committee*

is that we could use nuclear weapons in Europe and that the Soviets in all probability would not respond to nuclear weapons?

Gen. Goodpaster: I would not go so far as to say in all probability. I think you have to think probabilities, but I think there is an appreciable probability that they would not.[56]

As to the implementation of any strategy for the controlled, limited application of tactical nuclear weapons against a Pact attack, the conditions for actual employment, the nature and extent of such employment, and the doctrine for employment after any Soviet use, remain—a quarter of a century after the introduction of TNW to NATO—to be spelled out. The initial decision to respond with nuclear weapons hinges on the qualification "if necessary," and necessity is itself far more a matter of political decisionmaking than of military judgment.

NATO's Council and Defense Planning Committee provide the normal forum consultation and, in principle, would deliberate on the political and military objectives of proposed tactical nuclear employment, the methods of employment, and the consequences of a decision for or against employment. When these deliberations have been concluded, the views of the member nations are transmitted to the nuclear power possessing the weapons proposed for employment and the decision of the nuclear power is then conveyed to the NATO governments, the North Atlantic Council, and the major NATO commanders for final concurrence.

Clearly this consultation process is hardly amenable to decisions being quickly reached. Considering the complexity of the decisionmaking problem, however "agonizing" any decision to use nuclear weapons may be, the agonies associated with ingesting and analyzing a mélange of considerations by such a diverse group of national leaders would seem great enough.

The most recent U.S. Army operational manual, *Operations*, FM 100-5 (July 1976), outlines the nature and time for a tactical nuclear release request sequence in NATO (see figure 1). If this procedure were indeed to govern TNW decisionmaking and release in time of war, (1) it seems highly doubtful that the weapons could be used effectively against many targets in a fluid ground war, and (2) it seems likely that the Soviets could intercept and preempt many of the communications.

In view of these observations, it may be more appropriate to de-

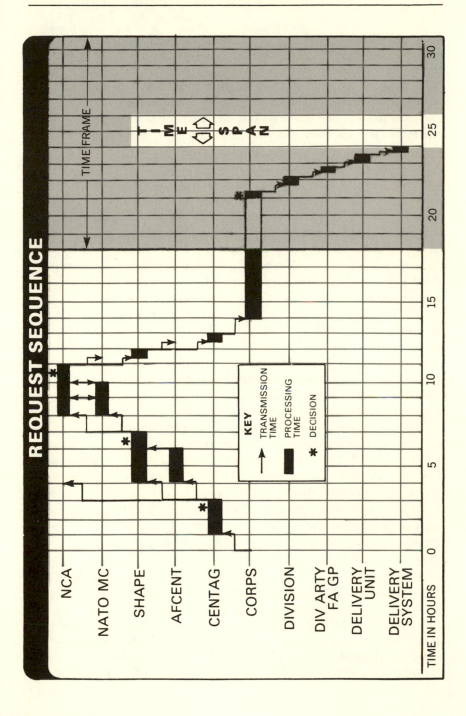

scribe the controlling factors for NATO's possible use of tactical nuclear weapons as much more a nebulous agreement to deal with an undefined contingency than a strategy or doctrine for use.

Ground force doctrine envelops the areas of planning, procedures, and techniques for waging conflict. In this regard, the doctrine covering the conventional forces of the United States and NATO *in a conventional conflict* is a fairly well established product. In the nuclear arena, however, there is little that can meaningfully be said about doctrine, since there is no real doctrine for employing tactical nuclear forces in a direct defense of territory. Initiation of the use of tactical nuclear weapons is determined more by politics and contingency than by doctrine or plans, and then is governed more by constraint than by military exigency; and, considering the almost impossible complexity of the decisionmaking process, it is shaped by factors that work essentially against, rather than for, an effective war-fighting capability.

The United States and NATO do not have what appropriately can be called a *doctrine* for tactical nuclear weapons and forces; nor in the current framework and climate is there likely to be one. Rather than spelling out terms of use, the current guidelines are basically concerned with conditions enabling (or preventing) a decision for use —with the military aspects of the problem almost submerged by the overriding procedural and political factors.

There is currently some progress, conceptually, in that these deficiencies are now officially acknowledged. That standards for modernization are now being set forth attests to the existence of the deficiencies. For example, the Department of Defense Nunn amendment report states: "NATO conventional forces *should* be able to operate satisfactorily in a nuclear environment. The theater nuclear forces *should* be capable of complementing the conventional forces in combined conventional nuclear operations. The force posture operational plans, and command and control *must* reflect this objective."[57] (Emphasis added.) This, however, is a statement of what *should be*, not what *is*, despite over twenty years of TNW deployment in Europe.

At the present time, the state of modernization of U.S.-NATO tactical nuclear capabilities reflects the doctrinal stagnation. The only new weapon system to enter the force since 1962 has been the Lance missile (deployed to NATO in 1974); but even here the dual-capable requirements imposed on the Lance design included the ability to deliver conventional munitions. As such, the payload capability had to be increased very substantially over that conforming solely to nuclear warhead delivery—in turn resulting in a much larger and more expensive system. (Even so, it is most questionable that Lance really has a respectable conventional option, in view of the weapon's delivery error.) Lance itself was a long-delayed program, and the result was a compromise weapon, optimum for neither a conventional nor a nuclear role. From this standpoint, the Lance system cannot truly be described as representing a deliberate effort toward tactical nuclear moderniza-ion. Rather, its development and deployment have been more along the lines of Secretary Schlesinger's description of resource allocation, namely: "Of the resources we invest in the general purpose forces, almost all go to conventional rather than to our tactical nuclear capabilities."[58]*

Beyond Lance, there is, at present, no indication that a new delivery system will soon be developed. There have been design studies that show that by incorporating advances in propulsion and ordnance technology, a highly effective, discriminate, and mobile battlefield nuclear missile could be available. However, at this juncture, there has been no announced decision by the Defense Department to undertake such development.

On the nuclear warhead side, there is little to indicate that since Schlesinger's observation in 1967 the tactical nuclear stockpile has undergone significant modernization. Congressional testimony in 1973 indicates that the incorporation of more advanced technologies, such as enhanced radiation, in the stockpile remained in the future. During testimony before the Joint Atomic Energy Committee, the following exchanges took place:

> Dr. Walske: With regard to nuclear artillery, a test relative to a concept for (deleted) this is a Livermore design, it produces, should produce, about a (deleted) yield which the laboratory estimates would be equivalent in terms of personnel kill to about a (deleted) weapon.
>
> Rep. Hosmer: These are the kinds of weapons that the letter that I sent to former Secretary of Defense, Clark Clifford, referred to. That was some considerable time ago. Is it not?

---

*And President Carter's proposed military budget for FY 1979 would increase this disparity even more, having as a principal objective the improvement and even increase of U.S. *conventional* forces in Western Europe.

Dr. Walske: Yes. This is not a weapon yet . . . I think that, for future development, it is a possibility. It is not in hand at the moment, but is certainly a possibility. . . .

Sen. Symington: Do you know if the Department of Defense is giving any consideration to developing low-yield anti-personnel battlefield weapons which depend on enhanced neutron radiation as a kill mechanism?

Dr. Walske: Yes, we are. That is discussed in the Development Guidance as an area of interest for the Department of Defense. . . . While in the past there had been quite a burst of enthusiasm for enhanced radiation weapons, uncertainty that developed in the area of biological effects did slow down the interest in it, but a good bit of interest exists today in the area.[59]

As of this writing, although the President has stated that "we must retain and modernize our theater nuclear capabilities," the issue of such modernization has not been promoted by the Carter administration. The administration's decision on ER remains held in abeyance (after an attempt to place the responsibility—or onus—on Allied governments), and it is not yet known whether modernization will win out over antinuclear tendencies. Past comments by key members of the administration may or may not provide a guide. However, Mr. Warnke, director of the U.S. Arms Control and Disarmament Agency, has been especially outspoken in his opposition to such modernization, telling Congress in 1974:

I would like to discuss briefly the problem that I see in the suggestion that perhaps we might develop a new generation of smaller, neater, and cleaner tactical nuclear weapons . . . it seems to me that the development of such a new generation of tactical nuclear weapons would be an absolute disaster. I think that it would be, first, the most extreme financial improvidence because of the billions of dollars of expense that would be necessary to develop this new generation of smaller nuclear weapons.

I believe, moreover, that the development and the replacement of existing tactical nuclear weapons with these weapons that might have lower yield and greater accuracy and presumably fewer collateral damage consequences would erode rather than strengthen deterrence.

For these reasons, I am unwaveringly opposed to the development of a new generation of tactical nuclear weapons which would have lower yield, greater accuracy, and fewer collateral consequences.[60]

If this view were to hold it would represent continuation of those policies adopted in the early 1960s in spite of the many changes that have since occurred. It would also ignore entirely the adversary side of the equation.

The Soviet Side

At about the time that the Kennedy administration changed U.S. policy away from tactical nuclear weapons, the Soviet Union moved doctrinally to place primary reliance on nuclear weapons. Nuclear weapons came to be regarded as the mainstay not only of strategic forces' firepower but also of Soviet ground forces' firepower. The expansion of Soviet general purpose conventional forces in recent years has not been a move toward a Western-style conventional emphasis philosophy; rather it has been accompanied by an expansion of tactical nuclear capabilities and has represented a marrying of nuclear and nonnuclear capabilities to achieve truly general purpose forces.

As has been reiterated by Marshal Grechko, the products of nuclear weapon research "have become the determining factor in the revolutionary changes in military affairs." In delivery systems, the USSR has concentrated on the development and modernization of systems fundamentally for nuclear operations. Dual-capability criteria for efficient utilization of conventional warheads by these weapons, in contrast to the U.S. approach, do not appear to have been important.

Soviet doctrine emphasizes the importance of *surprise initiative,* and uninterrupted *momentum.* Though it is portrayed defensively in training exercises, it very quickly asserts itself as highly offensive, based principally upon blitzkrieg armored movements exploiting the use of nuclear weapons against the enemy. While the Soviets, naturally, deny in their writing that they are the aggressors, their literature emphasizes the offensive and reiterates consistently that upon sensing that an enemy attack is about to be launched, preemption and seizure of the initiative are essential. It is difficult to exaggerate the role and objective of surprise in Soviet doctrine. The Soviets appear quite willing, even, to forego advantages of preparation and concentration, to a degree apparently difficult to accept in the West, in order to achieve surprise. To that end, operational principles of deception are expected to play a major role.

In contrast to the Western basis for planning, the expectation that the Soviet strategy includes a protracted period of mobilizing their forces prior to combat, Marshal Grechko has written:

> The time factor has particular significance in combat readiness. During the wars of the past, rather extended times were given for bringing the troops into a state of readiness. At present the enormous speed of the missiles and aircraft requires that the troops be brought into a state of full combat readiness in literally a few minutes. Only under this condition can we count on the effective repelling or thwarting of surprise attacks by the aggressor and the successful execution of combat missions.[61]

The following quotations are typical of consistent statements in Soviet literature on the importance (and expected use) of nuclear weapons in surprise attacks, seizing the initiative, and mounting the offensive:

> . . . use of nuclear weapons has further emphasized the role of the offensive as a decisive form of military action, even giving rise to the necessity to solve defensive tasks by means of active offensive operations.[62] (Lt. Gen. I. Zavyalov)

> The employment of nuclear weapons has greatly increased the role and significance of surprise in combat and has raised the requirement for its attainment.[63] (Maj. Gen. I. E. Krupchenko)

> To attain the greatest effectiveness, it is recommended that the nuclear strikes be launched at the start of the firepower preparation unexpectedly for the enemy. Preemption in launching a nuclear strike is expected to be the decisive condition for the attainment of superiority over him and the seizure and retention of the initiative.[64] (Col. A. A. Sidorenko)

> Equipping the Soviet Army and Navy with nuclear weapons and other combat equipment greatly increased their fire and striking power. . . . Nuclear weapons have made fundamental changes in military affairs. This weapon, as the most effective and powerful one, is the primary means of destroying the enemy. Its use . . . is expected to insure the rapid achievement of strategic results at the very start of combat actions. . . . What is more, the use of nuclear weapons sharply increased the combat capability of ground forces and offers them extensive new opportunities for waging active offensive operations.[65] (Chief Marshal P. A. Rotmistrov)

Relative to U.S.-NATO ambivalence toward the employment of TNW, the Soviets have expressed forcefully the basic elements of a true nuclear doctrine and strategy. Operations are predicated on the use of nuclear strikes to create the conditions for exploitation of mobile armor and infantry units in combination with airborne forces; this to be accompanied by—or even preceded by, if deemed necessary—a preemptive strike on NATO's means of nuclear delivery. Striking first and hardest in an attempt to disrupt the enemy at the outset is basic to Soviet operational planning. Emphasizing the requirement for continually maintaining the offensive, operational strategy calls for rapid day and night movement of maneuver forces in combined arms operations to sustain the initiative attained at the outset:

> *The art of conducting military operations with the use of nuclear weapons and that of employing conventional forces have many fundamental differences. But they are not in opposition, are not mutually exclusive, and are not isolated one from the other; on the contrary, they are closely correlated and are developing as a single body.*[66]

> *The path for the advance of the troops will be cleared by nuclear weapons.*[67]

> *Modern motorized rifle troops equipped with armored vehicles of high trafficability are capable of accomplishing marches over great distances quickly, entering the battle from the march and conducting it without dismounting in close coordination with the tanks . . . forcing water obstacles . . . and developing the offensive at high rates right after nuclear bursts.*[68]

> *In recent years, the Airborne Troops have developed rapidly. Their mission is to wage combat in the enemy rear using nuclear attack means, to make rapid use of the results of nuclear strikes against enemy objectives located deep in the rear.*[69]

Based upon what can be determined from Soviet statements of their own doctrine, there is little to indicate that the official appraisal that forms the basis for NATO's planning and posture is well founded. While many political officials and military planners disagree with the threat premises of NATO's planning, and while some, such as Britain's former defense minister, Denis Healey, have spoken out (as follows), they remain unheeded.

> *I don't think it would, in fact, make sense for NATO to aim at an all-out conventional defense against an all-out Warsaw Pact conventional*

attack because all Soviet exercises and training assume the use of nuclear weapons from the word "go," so I think an all-out conventional attack is very unlikely. . . . The other side would use nuclear weapons to begin with: there's a great deal of evidence for that, both in the exercises they do and in their strategic journals.[70]

That the Soviets' strategy foresees an essential role for a strong conventional weapons capability is acknowledged in their military writings. Indeed, considering the very substantial Soviet conventional force capabilities, that is to be expected. However, in the context of high-intensity ground war with the West, references to nonnuclear employment are generally coupled with statements about the decisiveness of nuclear strikes, the importance of *combined* nuclear and nonnuclear arms operations, and the conduct of conventional operations with a view toward nuclear strikes; and solely conventional operations are associated with smaller unit operations exclusively.

The following quotations are examples of Soviet views on the importance of nuclear weapons:

Nuclear missiles will be the decisive means of armed combat. Along with this, conventional weapons will also find use, and under certain conditions, the units and subunits can conduct actions solely with conventional means.[71]

Conventional weapons have not lost their importance; they occupy an important place in the overall material-technological base of the Armed Forces. Therefore, they have a right to existence. But, of course, they must be improved applicable to new conditions and new demands of warfare. . . .

The development of nuclear weapons caused qualitative changes in the methods and forms of combat operations and introduced many new factors into the principle of concentration. In the past, massing was expressed in a physical concentration of men and weapons along narrow axes. This created the requisite superiority over the enemy and ensured successful execution of the combat mission in the selected sector. Now it has become very dangerous to effect a large concentration of men and equipment in a small area. At the same time, it has become possible to apply the massed efforts of heavy firepower scattered over a large area.

The massed employment of nuclear weapons and other firepower, as well as the high density of tanks and other combat vehicles in combined-arms major units, produce sharp changes in the situation. Troops should

> *be able to concentrate rapidly in order to launch a powerful attack on the enemy, and they must be able to disperse just as swiftly, in order not to present a convenient target for a nuclear strike. . . . The conflict between concentration and dispersal of forces is resolved by increasing force mobility.*[72]

> *One must assume that, even in the conduct of military operations with conventional armaments . . . the main thing that will influence the mode of operation of the troops will be the continual threat of nuclear weapons. From this fact derives the most important task—to teach the troops to operate either with or without the use of nuclear weapons—to achieve a rapid changeover from one form of operations to the other, from fighting with conventional weapons to conditions of nuclear weapons.*[73]

There is every indication that the Soviets are serious about military operations in a nuclear environment: their doctrinal writings focus on it, their training is oriented to it, and their organization and equipment reflect it. Much of the Soviet military equipment, such as tanks and armored personnel carriers provided to the Middle East nations and captured during the October War, were equipped with nuclear effects sensors and instructions for operating in a nuclear environment. The keen Soviet interest in tanks and tank warfare is based not only on Soviet blitzkrieg operations but also—according to the manual *Vremya i Tanki*—on advantages in nuclear warfare:

> *As post-war exercises have shown, tanks are more suited than other types of military equipment to combat actions where nuclear weapons are used. In particular, they are suited to enduring powerful dynamic loads. The advantage of the tank is that its armor protects the crew against light radiation and decreases the effect of penetrating radiation, while the tank's actual weight gives it stability which protects it against the shock wave. As a result of this, the use of tanks under conditions where nuclear weapons have been employed makes it possible to wage active combat action immediately after the nuclear explosion on contaminated terrain.*
>
> *Thus, the conclusion can be drawn that the appearance of nuclear weapons not only failed to diminish, but, on the contrary, only strengthened the role of the tank in battle.*[74]

As this quotation implies, Soviet doctrine for major use of tanks (such as in a NATO-Pact conflict) views their use primarily in the context of nuclear conflict, actual or potential, where they play a complementary role to the primary nuclear role.

"Nuclear missile war" seems to connote theater-wide employment of nuclear weapons in some depth against main enemy targets, quite possibly involving a "preemptive" move when the Soviets (ostensibly) believe NATO to be about to resort to massive use of nuclear weapons. However, the emphasis on a nuclear environment is so prevalent in Soviet discussions of operations that it seems almost certain that the Soviets have not excluded from "conventional" tactics and operations the battlefield employment of nuclear weapons to promote penetration and breakthrough. Supporting this observation is the apparent introduction of nuclear artillery into the Soviet ground forces.

It should also be kept in mind that while the Soviets revere the military revolution wrought by nuclear weapons, they apparently do not attach the same enormous political-psychological distinction that the West does to nuclear versus nonnuclear weapons. (Nuclear escalation, of course, may occur, and it is discussed in Soviet writings, but escalation is not by definition the using of nuclear weapons.) To the Soviets, the nature of a war is determined and distinguished first and foremost by the political objectives and implications involved, not by the use or nonuse of nuclear weapons. This view was expressed in *Red Star*:

> Of course, all this does not mean that there is no qualitative difference between nuclear-missile warfare and warfare waged by conventional means. But the objective scholar is obliged to follow general moral criteria for assessing war, depending not on the technical means with which it is waged but on the political aims which it serves.[75]

The book *The Philosophical Heritage of V. I. Lenin and Problems of Contemporary War* takes great issue with those Western writers who consider the nature of war to be determined by the use or nonuse of nuclear weapons and who allege that nuclear use changes the basic political essence of warfare:

> Techniques and methods of falsification of the essence of war, couched in "nuclear" terms, have become quite widespread. They are permeated with the spirit of relativism and sophistry, a pseudo-innovative approach to this problem. Manifested in them is a nihilistic attitude toward theory and past experience, an anarchistic rejection of theses and conclusions reached in the prenuclear age, as well as an inability to interpret new phenomena from the standpoint of genuine science.

> *Referring to the development of nuclear missile weapons, the ideologues of imperialism are attempting to torpedo Marxist-Leninist theses which reveal the link between politics and war, to belittle their cognitive value for the "nuclear age." They declare that the new weapon has radically and fundamentally altered the relationship between politics and war, has disrupted the correlation between them which has developed over many centuries, and has made obsolete the formula of war as a continuation of politics by violent means.*

> *Although the development of this new weapon does introduce substantial changes into the correlation between politics and war, it does not eliminate the relationship between them. . . . Thus, the relationship between politics and war, thoroughly revealed in the writings of Lenin, not only remains valid in the Nuclear Age, but acquires even greater significance.*[76]

Thus, as seen by the Soviets, nuclear weapons are a new, more destructive, and more efficient technical means of waging war, but the nature of a war is still determined by politics.

It should also be kept in mind that a major Soviet nonnuclear offensive—particularly if it did require lengthy and visible mobilization prior to attack, as U.S.-NATO planning would have it—would maximize NATO's ability to mobilize for its defense and would permit it to disperse its nuclear warheads and delivery systems, which are normally stored at a relatively small number of sites highly vulnerable to nuclear attack.* By such a strategy, the Soviets—in what would be an unprecedented show of military cooperation—would be promoting NATO's defensive capability and placing the Soviet offensive in jeopardy.

In view of what the Soviets generally emphasize regarding doctrine and strategy for their ground forces, one may wonder what the underlying reasons are for NATO's conventional emphasis strategy. That there should be a difference in strategy by the two sides is not surprising; but that no apparent credibility is given by the U.S.-NATO side to the veracity of the expressed Soviet viewpoint seems curious.

In summing up an evaluation of Soviet strategy and doctrine for their ground forces, Britain's military analyst, John Erickson, concluded:

---

*Even after dispersal, it is likely that a substantial fraction of weapons would remain in these sites. (*Setting National Priorities: The 1972 Budget* (Washington, D.C.: Brookings Institution, 1971), p. 99.) Current dispersal plans and procedures, founded on the same planning assumption of a conventional attack, require reevaluation and, no doubt, revision for nuclear attack contingencies.

The orientation was, and is, basically nuclear: certainly the notion of conflict at any level of weapons employment has been admitted, but there has been little, if any, change in the broad-based Soviet feeling that any conflict seriously joined in Europe could scarcely be kept within the kind of "limits" which American theorists tended to purvey. The Soviet view of "flexible response" as enunciated by NATO was one of ill-concealed skepticism, either about the feasibility of holding on the lid at the conventional level or the employment of tactical nuclear weapons in "selective" fashion. As for the elaborations of the basic principles underlying likely Soviet practice, these have been subject to a number of sophisticated glosses, but no basic revision. Perhaps the only significant change in the past year or so has been the hint—and not much more—that a form of nuclear preemption might lie behind the military's logic, that the "surprise factor" can be augmented by secrecy, that the Soviet forces are inexorably committed to the seizure of the initiative at the earliest possible moment, and that high-speed offensive operations to exploit the full depth of the European theater demand even greater prominence for the armored and airborne forces available to the Soviet command. . . . The emphasis and the focus remains pronouncedly "nuclear": it was perhaps symbolic but no less telling that during the "conventional" operation in Czechoslovakia Soviet units moved in tactical missiles—a sign for all to see for all eventualities.[77] *(Emphasis in original)*

Again, referring to Schlesinger's Nunn amendment report, observations quite similar to those of Erickson are made in a Department of Defense report:

WP forces, current doctrine and training indicate a readiness, however, for conducting war in Europe with theater-wide, large scale nuclear strikes. Their large armored forces are postured to exploit these nuclear attacks with rapid, massive penetrations. . . .

The WP does not think of conventional and nuclear war as separate entities. Despite a recent trend to improve its conventional forces and to recognize that a conventional war in Europe need not escalate to nuclear war, the WP strategy, doctrine, and forces are still strongly oriented toward nuclear operations. . . .

While there are indications that WP strategists have accepted the concept of a possible initial conventional phase, WP forces are in fact postured and trained for theater-wide nuclear strikes against NATO nuclear and conventional military forces and for follow-on attacks by their armored conventional forces to exploit the nuclear attack and rapidly seize NATO territory.[78]

Erickson's remarks require some elaboration. They should not be taken to suggest that the Soviets have no options short of essentially unlimited use or that the Soviets have neither the capability, nor the interest, nor the operational plans for waging limited and selective nuclear warfare. At one time, open Soviet military literature was dominated by writing to the effect that nuclear warfare would not be limited or selective warfare but would assume widespread, even indiscriminate, general war characteristics.* Even then, however, Soviet literature did not exclude the possibility that quick military victory would obviate or reduce the possibilities of escalation, even when nuclear weapons were used to produce the victory. This is what one observer termed the *"fait accompli* approach."[79] Moreover, it seems clear that Soviet targeting is directed at military targets and probably those military targets crucial at the time to their objectives. This implies selectivity, however widespread the use.

Since then, with the development of Soviet capabilities and military flexibility, references to the inevitability of nuclear war escalation, and to the impossibility or improbability of keeping nuclear war within definable bounds, have begun to be replaced in Soviet military literature and exercises either by silence on the subject, or by explicit references to boundaries and to possible limitations in theater or local war. Soviet concern with specific targets according to political-military objectives, and even with limiting damage to assets in enemy territory that might become useful, has already been noted. Soviet ideology does not regard war as a suspension of politics but as a continuation, and political objectives may require specific controls. As stated officially by Secretary Schlesinger:

> In their exercises, the Soviets have indicated far greater interest in the notions of controlled nuclear war and non-nuclear war than has ever before been reflected in Soviet doctrine. As I indicated earlier, I think the doctrine is undergoing change.[80]

Not so curiously, since indications of Soviet interest in, and improved capabilities for, greater operational flexibility and limited conflicts in terms of control and target selectivity seem to have increased, many in the West interpret this to be interest in *non*nuclear theater warfare and in avoiding nuclear initiatives, and they argue that the

---

*That this was intended principally for Western audiences is strongly suggested by the influence given throughout the 1960s on problems of selective and controlled nuclear targeting by the classified journal of the Soviet General Staff, *Voyennaya Mysl'*, as illustrated by the quotations introduced earlier.

Soviets maintain a conventional emphasis, nuclear-weapons-are-escala-
tory point of view similar to that in the West.

It is clear that Soviet conventional capabilities have been drastically
improved, and it is now officially acknowledged in the West that Soviet-
Pact forces in Eastern Europe are capable of launching an assault
without the intensive buildup—and warning—envisioned in the 1960s.
Because of this capability, also, many interpret the threat as nonnuclear.
President Carter's pledge to improve NATO's defensive capabilities is
solely in terms of conventional capabilities against a conventionally
interpreted threat. This seems a perverse kind of wishful thinking. The
Soviets have not deviated from their emphasis on nuclear operations,
or rather combined arms operations involving both nuclear and nonnuclear forces simultaneously; and, in fact, all improvements in conventional firepower and equipment apply as well to a nuclear battlefield and seem clearly meant to supplement combined arms operations.
The Soviets have decidedly not adopted the Western view of nuclear
weapons.

One of the basic differences between the West and the Soviet Union
is that the West has most generally regarded the nuclear weapon as a
punitive-retaliatory deterrent, if not a weapon of totality whose use
should be avoided except as a last resort. This view has prevented the
West from incorporating nuclear weapons very effectively into its
doctrine of combat. In contrast, the Soviets have long regarded nuclear weapons as revolutionary for military operations and have sought
to adapt this basic appreciation of the weapons and their range of
effects into a "scientifically" worked-out war-fighting and winning doctrine—on both the tactical-battlefield and strategic-exchange levels. The
Soviet military may not reject the possibility of nonnuclear combat, and
they certainly do not take conventional forces lightly, working them
into their offensive doctrine even in a nuclear environment, but they
do place emphasis on combined conventional-nuclear operations, the
war-fighting virtues of nuclear weapons, and the nuclear orientation
of a modernized military doctrine. As Marshal Grechko put it:

> Work has begun on a broad complex of questions concerning the con-
> duct of combat operations under conditions involving the use of both
> nuclear and improved types of conventional weapons. The equipping of
> all the branches of the armed forces with nuclear missile weapons brought

forth the need for thoroughly reviewing the various concepts regarding the nature of a possible war.[81]

This is not the same as saying that Soviet doctrine is based upon indiscriminate use of nuclear weapons or that it recognizes no important distinctions and limitations on nuclear usage. To the contrary. Selective employment of nuclear weapons, closely tied to defined political and military objectives seems part of the Soviet approach: more than the West, which itself emphasizes highly-destructive and escalatory properties of nuclear weapons, the Soviets emphasize the increased effectiveness of nuclear weapons for traditional war-fighting purposes. Thus, the Soviets, perhaps polemically, criticize Western strategies as being overly obsessed with enormous civil destructiveness.

Soviet doctrine does not explicitly exclude local or limited wars in which nuclear weapons will be used tactically or even in which nuclear weapons may not be used. It is rather clearly their expectation that at least any relatively large-scale military conflict (that is, war with NATO) will involve the use of nuclear weapons, and it seems clear that their own decision on nuclear use will be governed by the situation and by military expediency. It is possible, however, that they recognize and plan to take advantage of the profound distinction the West places between nonnuclear and nuclear weapons, and the concomitant Western desire—nearly an overriding one—to avoid any nuclear use. They may appreciate that NATO has been unable to incorporate nuclear-weapons use into its combat doctrine and that it may be unable to implement whatever use is planned in a very timely and effective manner.

While remaining strongly nuclear-oriented and retaining an emphasis on timely, even "preemptive," nuclear strikes against the most lucrative and critical enemy military targets, Soviet thought on theater warfare (both operations and tactics), may have experienced some evolution—as their own capabilities have developed and changed, as exercises and study have explored variations, and as the Soviet assessment of the United States and NATO's posture, capability, and plans has changed.

It can be argued that by so openly expressing their views, the Soviets are really attempting to mislead the West. However, were this the case, they would at the same time be misleading themselves on a rather large scale. Also, the logic behind such a plot would be questionable, to say the least, for if they were to fully succeed, the result might be a change in NATO strategy toward a nuclear emphasis, in which case the Soviets would face a far more effective defense.

Western Sovietologists, noting the long-standing intolerance of the leadership for those who openly deviate from official state doctrinal principles, generally believe these declaratory statements to be truly representative of actual military doctrine.* Moreover, the Soviets themselves have expressed indignation that some Western analysts would doubt the veracity of such consistently expressed doctrines. For example, a statement made in 1974 by the late Marshal Grechko:

> Soviet military doctrine is attracting great attention in capitalist countries. A great number of books and articles are published on this theme and many lectures read. Some of the authors, falsifying events and facts, try to discredit Soviet military doctrine, to form a false opinion about it.
>
> We have never hidden and are not hiding the basic principal positions of our military doctrine. They are expressed with utmost clarity in the policies of the Communist Party and the Soviet government, in the state of our Armed Forces.[82]

On this issue, Benjamin Lambeth, an analyst then with the U.S. Central Intelligence Agency, observed:

> There are sharp limits beyond which the Soviets cannot go in their efforts to structure foreign audience perceptions simply through rhetorical fiat. It is important to bear in mind in this regard that Soviet military doctrine is not primarily a set of carefully contrived external propaganda poses but an important body of functional operating principles for internal consumption by the Soviet military. Since the Soviet military leadership can scarcely afford to lie to its own officer corps about its strategic intentions and objectives merely to deceive the West and, since the size and complexity of the Soviet political-military infrastructure preclude the communication of policy guidelines solely through secret channels, it should only stand to reason that the bulk of declared Soviet military doctrine should reflect a reasonably faithful image of actual Soviet strategic thinking.[83]

*"The members of the ruling hierarchy provide, through their public utterances, a substantially accurate picture of what they are up to and why, at least in a strategic sense. This is due to the requirement for uniformity that is so vital to the Soviet political system. Not only must those at the top speak with a single voice, but the entire hierarchy must echo that voice." (Foy Kohler, Mose L. Harvey, Leon Gouré, and Richard Soll, *Soviet Strategy for the Seventies: From Cold War to Peaceful Coexistence* [University of Miami Center for Advanced International Studies, 1973], p. 5. Also see W. R. Van Cleave, "Soviet Doctrine and Strategy: A Developing American View," in Lawrence Whetten, ed., *The Future of Soviet Military Power* [Crane, Russak: New York, 1976].)

That U.S.-NATO strategy has been predicated on what appears to have been a projection of a *U.S.-NATO preferred* strategy to the Soviets, seems strongly to be the case. If this is not the case, however, where is the evidence that the Soviets harbor a strategy that justifies a retention of NATO's?

Tactical Nuclear Force Postures

Of the resources we invest in the general purpose forces, almost all go to conventional rather than to our tactical nuclear capabilities. In part, this is so because many of our delivery systems—artillery, short-range missiles, and tactical aircraft—are dual-capable and, therefore, the distinction between their nuclear and their conventional role is not clear cut. But in greater part, it is because our forces, in their conventional role, can be used more flexibly, and contribute more to our critical defense posture and to the worldwide military equilibrium we seek. . . .

Why then do we maintain such large and diversified nuclear capabilities in our main theater commands? The answer is threefold. First, maintaining these capabilities is essential to deterrence so long as opposing forces maintain similar capabilities. They help to deter a limited first-use of nuclear weapons by an opponent and along with the conventional and nuclear forces help create a general deterrent against either conventional or nuclear aggression. Second, should deterrence fail, the tactical nuclear capabilities provide a source of nuclear options for defense other than the use of the strategic force. Third, given our doctrine of flexible response, we do not preclude the use of nuclear weapons by the United States and its allies in order to prevent a successful aggression.[84] (James R. Schlesinger)

The successes of the socialist economy and the outstanding scientific and technical achievements have made it possible to equip our Armed Forces with modern weapons and military material. This has led to fundamental changes in the armament of the Army and Navy and to changes in the organizational structure of the Armed Forces, in the views of the ways and forms for conducting combat operations. . . .

Nuclear missiles will be the decisive means of armed combat. Along with this conventional weapons will also find use and under certain conditions the units and subunits can conduct actions solely with conventional means.[85] (A. A. Grechko)

Although these two appraisals do not relate directly to specific tactical-nuclear-force-posture elements, they do serve to illuminate the subject in terms of how it is approached by both sides.

In comparing forces and postures it is essential not to mask the other's capabilities in comparisons based upon one's own doctrine and to try to see how his capabilities fit *his* doctrine. Nonetheless, mirror-imaging the threat is a characteristic deeply ingrained in Western thinking. Warsaw Pact forces are too frequently interpreted in the terms of Western doctrine, in terms of how they must operate (or fail) according to Western concepts. Differences in Pact-force capabilities often tend to be described as weaknesses simply because they would be regarded as such according to requirements stipulated by Western doctrine. Hence, Pact logistics capabilities are measured according to a Western view of protracted conventional operations (or conventional artillery assaults described as necessary by Western operations analysts). This is also true of the TNW part of the equation.

Yet, on the NATO side, it is inappropriate to talk about a tactical nuclear force posture. Western forces are structured and deployed basically on the premise that aggression against NATO will be non-nuclear and, therefore, the emphasis—in training, resources, and the peacetime-force posture—is on conventional war-fighting operations. NATO's TNW, which can hardly be described as a component of a tactical nuclear *force*, represent in effect an "add-on" to a conventional force. In only a very limited sense is a TNW war-fighting role planned or envisaged for them.

This is not to suggest that some military commanders may not attempt to use what they have for war fighting or that there is *no* military grappling with concepts for use of tactical nuclear weapons. The U.S. Army has been working diligently in this area toward examining new deployment and employment policies and concepts. However, there is no evidence that such examination has succeeded in overcoming the basic political resistance, and there seems to have been no substantial change in U.S. tactical-nuclear doctrine, strategy, or operations, or in the associated training and field exercises.

On the Soviet side, the force posture *can* be interpreted as being amenable to a strategy for any or all of the following: blitzkrieg conventional attack (without a mobilization period), surprise nuclear attack, and ongoing combined arms operations in a nuclear environment. All represent credible Soviet options. However, as noted, the emphasis has been placed on combined nuclear/nonnuclear operations.

If the intent were to be nuclear, the large combat-ready Soviet-Pact force represents what Secretary Schlesinger has called "a very immediate and palpable threat to the Center Region."[86] Moreover the very extensive preparation of military forces, key Soviet elements in Eastern Europe (air bases, command centers, and so on), and Soviet equipment for nuclear combat indicates the potential for nuclear operations.

In the current context of NATO strategy, it is difficult to compare the force posture of each side meaningfully enough to assess the balance of nuclear capabilities. For some time, ironically, largely because of the early Western lead in TNW and largely because of the Soviet assault in SALT on alleged U.S. advantages in so-called forward based systems, the West lost sight of the enormous Soviet theater nuclear strength. In fact, as the director of the U.S. Arms Control and Disarmament Agency recently pointed out, the European theater nuclear confrontation is one "that is strongly in favor of the Soviet Union." Such Soviet forces today "confer a significant numerical advantage over the much smaller nuclear forces" on the Western side in the theater; and, in contrast to the West, "Russia's strength in regional nuclear bombers and missiles grows like a towering, dark cloud over Europe and Asia."[87]

Based upon any realistic comparison, it is abundantly clear that NATO's force posture is highly vulnerable and ill designed within a framework of nuclear attack. Comparing forces, however discouraging, hardly tells the story. As then Defense Minister Healey put it in criticizing the tendency merely to count and compare peacetime forces: "The most important disadvantage of simply counting . . . is that it ignores the advantage which the enemy could hope to gain in a surprise attack. . . . By exploiting the initiative the Warsaw Powers could expect to make very rapid advances into NATO territory."[88] It is in that framework that the doctrine and force posture of the West merits evaluation.

Yet, NATO does not have the plans, posture, or forces required to defend successfully against a Soviet nuclear/conventional blitzkrieg attack; while the plans, posture, and forces it has almost invite such an attack should a decision ever be made to attack.

Primarily for reasons of economy (and the vicissitudes of politics and history), NATO's tactical nuclear force elements are deployed during peacetime at a relatively small number of bases, casernes, and storage sites that are the most likely targets for enemy nuclear attack.*

---

*Schlesinger reported, "In their peacetime locations the nuclear weapons are vulnerable to attack by WP theater nuclear forces, as are almost all of NATO's military forces." Department of Defense, *The Theater Nuclear Force Posture in Europe*, p. 23.

Thus, the nuclear-capable aircraft are located on some tens of bases; the nuclear artillery rockets and missiles are kept in a small number of caserne areas; and the nuclear warheads are stored at what was said to be "over 100 special ammunition sites" (a number that has since been reduced),† many collocated with the airfields and casernes.

Singularly important, with respect to the vulnerability of NATO's tactical nuclear capability, are the warhead storage sites whose permanence, conspicuous markings, and radio communication facilities lead to a veritable certainty that their locations are known to the Soviets. Compared with the number of tactical nuclear launchers that might be deployed in Eastern Europe for use against NATO's tactical nuclear facilities, NATO tactical nuclear concentration on the continent is extremely high.‡ As a consequence, a surprise attack involving Soviet tactical nuclear missiles, plus some fraction of the nuclear-capable aircraft, against sites in Western and Southern Europe could readily result in the destruction of the bulk of NATO's tactical nuclear capabilities.

Except for eastern Turkey, the target coverage of only Scaleboard and Scud missiles against NATO TNW facilities is essentially complete from Eastern European countries. Adding theater strike aircraft capability (some of the aircraft have combat radii substantially in excess of Scaleboard's range) further exacerbates NATO's nuclear vulnerability problem.

These capabilities versus NATO's posture clearly cast doubt on the objectives of the nuclear component of NATO's force posture, "to deter a limited first-use of nuclear options for defense other than the use of the strategic forces."[89]

In the above target-coverage discussion, the potential coverage over nuclear-capable installations in France and the United Kingdom has been omitted. Such omission stems from the fact that these two countries possess their own independent strategic nuclear capabilities and pre-

---

†The number was released by a U.S. Senate staff report in 1973, which according to an official source has been reduced by 20 percent or more since that time. *U.S. Security Issues in Europe: Burden Sharing and Offset, MBFR and Nuclear Weapons.* Staff Report prepared for U.S. Senate Foreign Relations Committee, Subcommittee on U.S. Security Agreements and Commitments Abroad, December 2, 1973. Reduction of sites report in Communication of Assistant to the Secretary of Defense for Atomic Energy, D. R. Cotter, to Senator John O. Pastore, *Congressional Record* S7185 (April 30, 1975).

‡It should be noted that the same can be said for the critical C^3 elements of the NATO defense posture, which are concentrated, soft, and highly vulnerable to nuclear effects, and which lack prudent redundancy.

sent the problem to the USSR that Soviet nuclear warheads (whether tactical or strategic) impacting on French or British soil may provoke a strategic attack on Soviet soil. This, in turn, brings up the fundamental political issue having to do with the utility of national strategic nuclear forces as related to alliance problems. It also brings into focus the politics of nuclear weapon employment from three standpoints: (1) whether Soviet use would elicit the invocation of U.S. strategic nuclear guarantees, (2) whether NATO tactical nuclear use would—or should—be coupled with strategic release, and (3) whether tactical nuclear usage by both sides would escalate to strategic nuclear exchanges.

Tactical Nuclear Weapons Politics

As noted in chapter 2, beginning in the early 1960s, a decided change in the U.S. attitude on the use of tactical nuclear weapons took place. Essentially, this change was in the direction of dampening any meaningful war-fighting role for tactical nuclear weapons, relegating this role to conventional weaponry, and leaving a "deterrence-only" role whose efficacy was held to be enhanced through coupling with the punitive threat of strategic nuclear forces. (That this view has taken root in Europe is demonstrated by the recent defense "White Paper" issued by the Federal Republic of Germany, in which tactical forces are treated abstractly as deterrence-only forces, whereas the defensive or war-fighting role is reserved exclusively for conventional forces.[90]

In the strategic force realm, a growing apprehension over rapidly developing Soviet strategic capabilities has increased the ambivalence of U.S. strategic nuclear force coupling. However, there has been continued insistence by key NATO European allies that these guarantees are critical to the Alliance. It has also been maintained by the Allies that these guarantees still must constitute the military cornerstone of the Alliance. (See, again, the Federal Republic of Germany White Paper.)

Yet, at whatever level—strategic or tactical—the underlying premise of U.S. military policy has been the desire to avoid use of nuclear weapons. And if such avoidance is a central objective at the tactical level one must suspect that it is paramount at the strategic level. It is clear that, despite early recognition of their potential, TNWs continue to be viewed as dangerous and highly unacceptable substitutions for conventional weapons, *even* if they should promise a less costly defense:

> *At the same time, I must stress that our tactical nuclear systems do not now and are most unlikely in the future to constitute a serious substitute for a stalwart non-nuclear defense. In fact, . . . the decision to initiate the use of nuclear weapons—however small, clean, and precisely used they might be—would be the most agonizing that could face any national leader.*[91] *(James R. Schlesinger)*

> *We could adopt the position that any serious attempt to erode our interests by military means would be met by the tactical use of nuclear weapons. In fact, the U.S. took precisely that position at one time in the past. . . . However tempting this view, and* the lower defense budgets that it might promise *it is an illusion.*[92] *(Donald H. Rumsfeld, emphasis added.)*

Remarks such as these, coming from U.S. secretaries of defense, suggest strongly that the U.S. aversion to tactical nuclear weapon usage has little or nothing to do with possibilities for discriminate application or with economics. Moreover, the United States has projected this attitude to prospective enemies of the United States and to allies. It is somewhat ironic then that in the strategic nuclear domain the new U.S. targeting doctrine places much significance on more selective and limited nuclear options for use against Warsaw Pact (including even the USSR) targets on the behalf of allies in a purely theater-warfare context. In essence, it is hoped that extended strategic force deterrence will be enhanced through selective and discriminate strategic use options, which might be both decisive and nonescalatory, while little hope is expressed for this in the tactical nuclear domain.

Strategic Nuclear Policy

> *Sane national leaders do not initiate strategic nuclear war and thus commit their people to national suicide.*[93] *(Secretary of State William P. Rogers)*

> *The existence of nuclear weapons creates conditions that are unprecedented in history, in that a war under current circumstances could lead to the destruction of all civilized life as we know it.*[94] *(Secretary of State Henry A. Kissinger)*

> *The imperialist ideologies are trying to lull the vigilance of the world's people by having recourse to propaganda devices to the effect that there*

will be no victors in a future nuclear war. These false affirmations contradict the objective laws of history. . . . Victory in war . . . will be on the side of world socialism and all progressive mankind.[95] *(Marshal of the Soviet Union, N. I. Krylov)*

In the West, it has been an almost uncontested article of faith for years that there can be no winners in a strategic nuclear war between the United States and the USSR and that virtually inconceivable destruction would be an inevitable product. Strategic nuclear warfare was relegated to the unthinkable. On the Soviet side, however, strategic nuclear war with the United States has been depicted as a realistic possibility for which extensive preparations, including public conditioning, are not only warranted but mandatory. The official Soviet view is that limiting of damage and a war-fighting–war-winning strategy are possible and must be pursued as the highest national security priority. As former Deputy Secretary of Defense Paul H. Nitze recently pointed out, "Americans have thought throughout the last 30 years in terms of deterring nuclear war, with the debate centering on how much effort is necessary to maintain deterrence, to keep nuclear war unthinkable. In the Soviet Union, the view has been quite different. . . . Soviet leaders from the outset discounted the impact of nuclear weapons to their people."[96]

With these fundamental differences, two key questions come into focus: (1) How much should NATO planning and strategy be based on U.S. strategic nuclear guarantees, that is, on the threat of the U.S. initiating a possible strategic nuclear exchange with the USSR? (2) What are the probabilities that conflict in Europe will escalate—through actions of one or both sides—to a strategic exchange between the United States and the USSR?

With respect to U.S. strategic pledges to allies, with one exception, the President of the United States at the time of decision, no one can definitely assess the probability that these pledges would be met. The decision to employ U.S. strategic nuclear weapons at present rests solely with the U.S. president.[97] Therefore, one can only conjecture on a president's decision should the dreaded moment ever arrive.

Were (then Secretary of State) Rogers' assessment of strategic nuclear war descriptive of the U.S. view of any such conflict, then the credibility of strategic nuclear guarantees versus the USSR clearly would be extremely low or even nonexistent.

Apart from the plausibility of such consequences for the United States, the deterrent value of U.S. strategic forces against theater-only attacks rests on *Soviet* perceptions of the credibility and effectiveness of their employment and of the net outcome of any U.S.-Soviet exchange. The credibility might or might not be enhanced by more selectivity and more options. Secretary Schlesinger argued that these limited options have cast U.S. strategic guarantees into a different, more credible perspective:

> *The reason for the change in targeting doctrine is that we know that we can persuade the Soviet Union that we are prepared to implement that threat, whereas reliance on the assured destruction doctrine could well lead the Soviet Union to believe that we are not prepared to implement the threat. It is for that reason that the changes in targeting doctrine have successfully eliminated doubts about the coupling of U.S. strategic forces with the defense of Western Europe.*[98]

That reasoning remains a matter of dispute, both as to accuracy and to desirability as strategic policy. In addition, there is a question of whether such action would be at all beneficial to attacked NATO allies. Should the Soviet attack ensure the attainment of the Soviet-Pact ground force objectives within a very short period, whatever the effects of U.S. strategic strikes, they might bear little significant relationship to the situation in Western Europe.

If the strategic nuclear action took place sometime after a Soviet attack had been mounted, there is little promise that strategic strikes *against the Soviet Union* would benefit the NATO cause, while they would greatly risk escalation. The employment of strategic forces against Pact military targets *not* in Soviet territory might seem to reduce the latter risk and to bear a more direct relationship to the military conflict in Europe. However, their efficacy is still subject to serious question unless one believes the war will be a prolonged conflict with Soviet success dependent upon the survival of such targets or believes that the demonstration of willingness to employ strategic weapons will lead (where tactical nuclear demonstrations failed) to Soviet cease-fire.

Aside from whatever deterrent or wartime effect the threat of escalation to strategic forces might have on the Soviets, the basic question remains whether, all things considered, reliance on such a strategy may have a far greater self-deterrent effect on the United States. However

selective and limited the option, given current strategic nuclear rela-
tionships, there will be an enormous deterrent to any U.S. initiation of
strategic strikes that could result in Soviet strikes on the United States.*
Unless it is assumed that such U.S. strikes would persuade the Soviets
to stop all aggressive action (including a response on the United
States), or unless one assumes a war in which strategic strikes would
have military effect, without escalation to U.S.-Soviet strategic exchanges, there must be serious doubt about the desirability of attempting to couple U.S. strategic nuclear forces to a European conflict.

*Although it was President Nixon's strong dissatisfaction with being constrained to a single
strategic nuclear option (i.e., SIOP) that led to the formulation of the new limited strategic
options, Mr. Nixon himself raised doubts regarding an option that envisaged even a very limited
U.S.-USSR nuclear exchange, stating: "Today, any nuclear attack—no matter how small;
whether accidental, unauthorized, or by design; by a superpower or by a country with only a
primitive nuclear capability—would be a catastrophe for the U.S., no matter how devastating
our ability to retaliate." U.S., President, *U.S. Foreign Policy for the 1970's: A New Strategy for
Peace, A Report to the Congress by Richard Nixon, February 18, 1970* (Washington, D.C.:
Government Printing Office, 1970), p. 125.

Alternatives for NATO

The Soviet development of doctrine and strategy for tactical nuclear conflict has evolved in the face of a failure of the West to come to grips with such conflict. NATO, rather than preparing for the real threat,* has based its doctrine and strategy on a mirror-imaged conventional threat, gambling heavily on protracted nonnuclear conflict and the avoidance of the use of nuclear weapons, instead of on their effective employment.

What is fundamentally at issue is the probable nature of any deliberate, major Soviet attack. Put in another way, what threat—in the event of a deliberate, planned Pact attack—is it most reasonable to use for planning purposes? It seems clear that in the event of an attack involving nuclear weapons at the outset and without sufficient strategic warning for effective NATO preparations—that is to say, precisely that depicted by Soviet doctrine—NATO's ability to resist the advance of Soviet-Pact ground forces would be highly questionable. (Given the lack of tactical nuclear doctrine and the great uncertainty of timely

---

*As has been pointed out, this is due in large part to a lack of real training for the threat as posed by Soviet doctrine and capabilities. A courageous 1975 *Army* article by a Soviet specialist in DIA pointed this out very well: "The clarity of the threat and the absence of response to it in Army training are so evident. . . . There is a lack of effective Army policy. There is a lack of suitable training material. There is ignorance of the Soviet armed forces so profound that many officers have no idea of the extent of their lack of knowledge. As a result of these three factors, there does not appear to be even an institutional desire to solve the problem that so clearly exists." Lt. Col. Michael K. Stein, "Oh Red Threat, Where Are You Now that We Need You?" *Army* 25, no. 8 (August 1975), p. 1920.

nuclear release, and given as well the overall deficiencies in Western defense, NATO's ability to resist *any* blitzkrieg Pact attack that has the advantage of tactical surprise and initiative can be said to be highly questionable.) NATO has not planned and prepared for such an attack; yet, for all the reasons brought out in the previous section, such an attack is *at least* as plausible—probably even more so—as a major, or all-out, nonnuclear attack involving an extended period of Soviet-Pact mobilization.

Were NATO to redefine the Soviet-Pact threat along nuclear emphasis lines, it is still not clear that a new doctrine and a reposturing and reequipping of NATO's forces would occur. After all, it could be argued, NATO's posture seems to have fulfilled the desired objective to date, and resistance to major changes would be substantiated.

Insofar as political satisfaction with the status quo (inertia) is coupled with persistent Western views about tactical nuclear weapons, major changes seem very unlikely for NATO, whatever the facts of the situation. As Professor Bernard Brodie observed concerning the ingrained conventional emphasis approach of NATO:

> *Simple facts, however, do not normally impede messianic vision. What was a novel and radical doctrine 15 years ago has now, in the mid-1970s, become the conventional wisdom of the interested public and of most of the defense community. Professional military officers tend today to be ambivalent on the matter. They usually are prepared in principle to use tactical nuclear weapons if the other side uses them first—or, as something of an afterthought, in case we find ourselves losing without them. But their thinking shows the results of 15 years of propagandizing by those bright and persuasive civilians who had the backing of strong Secretaries of Defense, including most recently Dr. James R. Schlesinger. They have, by the frank admission of some of them, simply not been thinking very much about it.**

However, since changed circumstances cannot always be ignored, such change cannot be dismissed as impossible. In the area of strategic nuclear forces, changes in the strategic balance, the undiminished determination of the USSR to expand and modernize its strategic capa-

---

*Dr. Brodie's view is summarized in his rhetorical question: "Can anyone believe, with confidence, that the Soviet Union would challenge us to so deadly a duel and yet leave the choice of weapons entirely to us?" *Toward a New Defense for NATO* (National Strategy Information Center, New York, 1976), p. 7

bilities, and clear, strongly held differences in Soviet strategic doctrine and concepts have *forced* changes in U.S. strategic thinking. For similar reasons, including a new recognition of deficiencies in NATO's ability to deter and defend, a similar situation may yet prevail in NATO.

To some extent, changes in U.S. strategic thinking have recently been reflected in statements of general objectives for NATO forces. The FY 1976 Department of Defense Report established as two objectives for improvements in NATO's theater nuclear forces that "the vulnerabilities of these forces to surprise nuclear attack should be reduced," and "selective, carefully controlled options" should be developed.[99] Elsewhere, Schlesinger also allowed that "NATO still needs improved doctrines for the tactical use of nuclear weapons."[100]

On the other hand, the emotions against matters nuclear in tactical or local limited war planning are so strong that changes in that direction may be resisted even in the face of strong evidence supporting such change. Unless there is a rational employment doctrine based upon a supportable posture, it is most unlikely that there will be change. During the series of congressional hearings since 1973 dealing with tactical nuclear weapons in NATO, that rational doctrine—as Schlesinger allowed—was apparently lacking. Congressional skepticism rather than enthusiasm concerning TNW modernization prevailed, reinforced by ample testimony that the role of TNW in defending Europe is highly limited and not based upon a war-fighting or defense capability. For example:

> *Tactical nuclear weapons have as their major if not only purpose the supplying of the logical bridge between conventional defense and the strategic nuclear deterrent. . . . The deterrent purpose of tactical weapons could abundantly be served by the maintenance of a few hundred at most.*[101] *(Paul C. Warnke)*

> *Tactical nuclear weapons cannot defend Western Europe; they can only destroy it . . . there is no such thing as tactical nuclear war in the sense of sustained purposive military operations. . . . I believe that all the useful purposes can be more than adequately served by 1000 tactical nuclear weapons. . . . The rest should be considered as candidates for removal either in order to enhance our conventional capability or to save money.*[102] *(Alain Enthoven)*

> *The Germans have become used to the presence of American nuclear weapons in Europe and they have come to see them as part of the deter-*

rent making it more credible that the United States would ultimately use strategic weapons. For this reason I do not believe that the United States should contemplate the withdrawal of all its nuclear weapons from Europe. I do believe, however, that it should be possible to make a substantial reduction in the number of nuclear weapons stationed in Europe.[103] *(Morton H. Halperin)*

Statements such as these are not conducive to any deliberate change in U.S. policy toward emphasis on tactical nuclear weapons. If anything they reflect a strong sentiment toward reducing drastically existing TNW capabilities in Europe.

Europeans quite naturally display little willingness to plan war in their homelands based upon the use of tactical nuclear weapons. These feelings have little to do with any studies of such conflict (or alternatives to it), of Soviet capabilities, or of prospects for refining TNW along discriminate lines. Rather, it is a visceral revulsion (but, nevertheless, a strong political fact of life) to nuclear warfare on one's own territory and this widespread attitude has had a profound effect on NATO's tactical nuclear policy.

But one can go a step further in asserting that there is an almost comparable revulsion to the thought of large-scale conventional war on their territory. European acquiescence to the U.S.-proposed conventional emphasis policy hardly has come readily and, although in 1967 (a half dozen years after the U.S. proposal) this policy was formally endorsed by NATO, by no means has it truly been accepted.

These feelings have led inexorably to a single-minded emphasis on, and faith in, "deterrence"—deterrence unencumbered by serious consideration of actual war fighting, especially nuclear war fighting:

For the Europeans, deterrence must be as absolute as possible because another major European war is unthinkable. Because of the hemorrhage of human lives and the physical devastation of the two World Wars, the advent of war is seen by them as inevitably their loss. Even success in fighting off a Soviet attack in a protracted conventional war is feared by them as the end of their society.[104] *(Paul Warnke)*

But the West Europeans, who fear the total destruction of their societies, should either a "classical" war à la World War II, or a limited nuclear war break out, see no acceptable alternative to making nuclear deterrence work. Consequently, (a) they tend to favor strategies that create the maxi-

*mum of uncertainty, and thus maintain the enemy's fear of escalation . . .;
(b) they are less than enthusiastic about devising "rational use" strategies
for the case of a failure of deterrence because none of these appears really
bearable.*[105] *(Stanley Hoffman)*

For all these reasons—which are primarily political and based more on the presumed apocalyptic nature of nuclear war (at any level) rather than on what few "facts" are available—possibilities for a greater emphasis on tactical nuclear strategies for NATO may seem remote. Moreover, it would appear that the years ahead will, most probably, be accompanied by cutbacks in NATO's nuclear arsenal.

During this period, it also can be expected that NATO's conventional strength will stay about the same—with possible manpower reductions compensated by other "teeth-to-tail" improvements—and its strategy will remain along conventional emphasis lines. However, the Soviet threat will not go away and NATO will, in effect, have swept a problem critical to its survival under the carpet.

At the root of the resistance to strategies with a greater tactical nuclear emphasis has been this ingrained aversion to crossing the nuclear firebreak. However, certain questions are permissible here: (1) Is the West's, and in particular Western Europe's, future truly less ominous if the nuclear firebreak remains uncrossed? (2) If it ever is crossed, would it be better for NATO to have discriminate, warfighting tactical nuclear options rather than what it now has? (3) Is basing policies on the attainment of such options really synonymous with making nuclear conflict more likely, or does it contribute more to deterrence? (4) Is the overriding objective deterrence, or the avoidance of any nuclear use? (5) Considering the importance of deterrence, in view of the greater deterrent effect from a military standpoint that a nuclear-postured NATO force would have, would such a force better serve Western Europe than the present conventionally oriented force? (6) Is it ultimately to the interest of either the United States or Western Europe to minimize local defense and base deterrence strategy on escalation to strategic exchanges? (7) Do the Soviets show a similar theological disposition against tactical nuclear weapons, as reflected by their policy and doctrine?

As to the first question, it has been, and continues to be, moot. All nuclear scenarios and their results are fraught with assumptions and speculation, as are such political prognoses. It is a question, however, that should be explicitly raised and considered.

As to the next few questions, a NATO force that is postured best to thwart the range of military strategies that the Soviets might hold certainly has a greater deterrent potential than the present posture, which can defend—most hopefully—only against nonnuclear aggression, and at that an aggression with ample warning and beset with internal failings. If, indeed, NATO Europe is concerned with no fighting, it must be concerned with war fighting. For deterrence, for defense, and for reduction of the destructiveness of a war, NATO must develop sensible TNW employment plans and procedures, weapons with highly discriminate capabilities, and improved civil defense measures. A posture so designed would seem to be more in the interests of European allies, for deterrence, and in the event of its failure, compared with the alternatives.

The last question has been dealt with extensively here: If the Soviets are so disposed toward the Western nuclear theology, it has not been apparent in their doctrine, their equipment and training, or other preparations apparent to the West.

Granting that change by the West in the direction of tactical nuclear emphasis seems unlikely in the foreseeable future, nevertheless, should this come about, what is the nature of the military alternatives based on such emphasis?

To begin with, were NATO's doctrine to be revised to take into account the serious possibilities of initial Soviet nuclear attack, by far the most pressing priority would be the requirement for a more survivable force posture—involving both nuclear and conventional elements.* The problem here is very much akin to that facing U.S. land-based strategic weapons, where the vulnerability of Minuteman missiles and B-52 bombers has become an increasingly serious prob-

---

*Although Schlesinger's Nunn amendment report regards a surprise nuclear attack on NATO as "very unlikely," it contains explicit recommendations for improving the survivability of NATO's weapons against such attack: "Survivability of NATO theater nuclear capabilities under both conventional and nuclear attack is a major requirement. This particularly means that alerted, dispersed units and their essential support (e.g., warheads, intelligence, logistics) should be survivable. . . . A theater nuclear force R&D program has been initiated with the following objectives: To assess the survivability of these elements under conventional and nuclear attack, identify deficiencies and develop improvements; to develop technology to counter possible future threats to the survivability of these theater nuclear elements." Department of Defense, *The Theater Nuclear Force Posture in Europe*, p. 20.

lem. A revamped force posture would call for one of greatly increased dispersal and mobility over that now existing. A change from that involving a comparatively few highly lucrative and vulnerable targets to one involving a greater number of targets, individually less lucrative, dispersed, concealed, mobile, or defended, would be necessary. For the fixed targets necessary and key to Western military capability, or to its peacetime maintenance, active defenses, evacuation, and redundancies should be prepared.

Before attempting to grapple with the specifics of an alternative force posture for NATO, a fundamental issue needs discussing. This has to do with the notion that a deterrent force can be designed on a "purely deterrent" basis rather than around the requirements for defense and a war-fighting capability. As is also the case for strategic forces, the difference in force posture for these different design points can, in principle, be very great.

With respect to a nuclear emphasis force posture planned and designed to maximize war-fighting capability, it should be realized that an intellectual vacuum, pertinent to this problem, now exists. Because of NATO's long-standing conventional emphasis there has been an overwhelming tendency to predicate official studies and analyses dealing with tactical nuclear weapons on nuclear engagements arising from initial conventional conflict. Consequently, practically all scenarios have involved nuclear battlefield conditions where the postures of both sides have been determined primarily by prior conventional conditions. The nature of a conflict, where both sides have planned for nuclear employment from the very beginning, has rarely been considered, let alone adequately assessed. As a consequence, the problem has been and remains (in Secretary McNamara's terms) a "vast unknown" and, as Senator Symington has pointed out, no comprehensive doctrine for such conflict has been officially formulated by the U.S. military.

We cannot conveniently or logically apply some of the cardinal principles of strategic nuclear deterrence to the tactical arena. Tactical nuclear weapons pose no direct threat to the Soviet Union, and thus we cannot ascribe a punitive retaliatory value to these weapons in the sense that we do toward justifying our strategic deterrent capability. Moreover, the Soviets might not feel at all constrained by Western threats to inflict high levels of damage against their Warsaw Pact allies, and

NATO Europe—not having a credible strategic deterrent—might well be self-deterred from such measures if it feared that such action would bring about a response in kind by the Soviet Union.*

If punitive retaliation does not fit so comfortably in the deterrent equation, then the problem boils down to the question of what fraction of NATO's force can survive the critical Soviet attack and hold the necessary responsiveness to thwart the Soviet aggressive objectives, to deny Western European territory to Pact forces. In other words, deterrence must be measured in terms of some level of residual defensive capability. As such, the question becomes, What is the level and how much less (*less* seems axiomatically correct) is it than that associated with a posture providing "optimum" war-fighting capability? Since a war-fighting capability intrinsically contains a deterrence capability but not necessarily the opposite, for the case of tactical nuclear warfare our essential ignorance on the subject turns a venerable axiom into a cliché.

But this question closes the circle since, for the reasons brought out above, there is no truly sound way to determine the force requirements for either posture and, thus, determine this differential. We are, in essence, concerned with combining two war-fighting postures—one of which poses sufficient uncertainty to the Soviet planner to dissuade him from aggression, that is, to achieve the conditions for deterrence; the other having the military capability to achieve the required military objective, that is, a successful forward defense.

The determination of an adequate tactical nuclear force posture for NATO entails a level of subjective judgment perhaps even greater than that applied to the analysis and evaluation of the strategic and conventional force areas (where it seems easier to disguise such judgment in quantitative analysis). For the time being, the analytical community cannot agree on a number of key military assumptions to permit any analytical assessment. When an apparently clear-cut military rationale is difficult to attain, political considerations become the dominant realities. (This has been particularly true for nuclear weapon issues.)

The political equation affecting these weapons, until very recently,

---

*France, of course, has long divorced itself from U.S.-NATO nuclear policy, giving every indication that it reserves the use of its nuclear weapons for its own national defense. Britain has said very little openly of any willingness to use its nuclear weapons against Soviet-Pact territory on behalf of continental allies, preferring to stress the indispensability of the U.S. nuclear umbrella.

has reflected acceptance of NATO's stockpile but has provided no real incentive for the modernization or reposturing of these weapons. And now, bolstered by the U.S. offer to withdraw unilaterally a thousand nuclear warheads from Europe in the context of MBFR (an implicit signal that there are at least that many warheads deployed that the Alliance can do without), congressional pressure to remove a good part of the stockpile may well be successful. Unfortunately, it is likely that such action will be taken without compensatory modernization of the remainder.

If NATO were to adopt a theater nuclear emphasis strategy based primarily upon tactical nuclear weapons in a defensive, denial role, what would be the structure of such a force and what weapon modernization objectives need to be pursued? The first requirement for a new force posture is the development of a doctrine for TNW combat, including TNW employment guidelines for preventing enemy seizure of territory without concomitant high levels of collateral damage. The primary responsibility for this must rest with the U.S. Army, but overall coordination with all services and with the principal NATO Allies involved is essential. Politics control. But Allied, particularly German, sensitivities to the idea of nuclear land warfare must not continue to be used as an excuse to do little. The lack of a sensible employment doctrine certainly contributes to resignation and even abhorrence concerning TNW defense. The latter then becomes a barrier to constructive Allied work on such a doctrine. This self-perpetuating situation must be changed by understanding the centrality of TNW defense to deterrence.

Another prerequisite is greater awareness within the military of the problems and opportunities of nuclear land warfare. The ostrich approach represented in the paucity of military training for nuclear combat is worse than senseless—it is irresponsible and an abrogation of military professionalism. Two decades ago an assistant commandant of the U.S. Army's Command and General Staff College laid it on the line:

> *If we believe the advent of nuclear weapons presents an insurmountable problem to the strategist, tactician, and logistician, we have begun to lose the flexibility and imagination without which we are doomed to defeat. If we accept this technological advancement as the greatest challenge in*

centuries of military operations, we can make this force the basis for the preservation of peace—or for victory in war if the need arises.[106]

The challenge has been largely ignored, and the consequences may ultimately be those predicted.

After the development of doctrine and the training of armed forces for nuclear combat, the major improvement necessary lies in NATO's force posture, which is exceedingly vulnerable to enemy nuclear attack. An overriding priority must be given to improving force survivability—against a surprise attack, as first priority, and then sustained operational survivability in combat. It seems obvious that the first step to be taken is to move away from the present system of dependence upon a relatively few fixed, unhardened, undefended and highly lucrative installations: major airfield complexes, major bases, and casernes where most troops and their equipment normally are situated, nuclear warhead storage sites, and central C^3 facilities—all of which could be destroyed in the initial stages of conflict, and, as situated today, with a relatively small number of strikes. What is necessary is a posture based upon a greater degree of dispersal and mobility, augmented by improved active and passive defenses, hardening, and C^3 redundancy, the extent of which would be a function of politics, geography, and economics as well as military logic. The goal would be to reduce vastly the effectiveness of a surprise attack and to make more difficult enemy reconnaissance and targeting in wartime.

Clearly, certain force elements are not widely dispersible. For example, one could consider increasing substantially the number of air bases and decreasing their value as targets, both to compound the Pact attack problem and to promote crisis stability (i.e., by decreasing major vulnerabilities in NATO strike forces). However, a very wide dispersal approaching a posture of only a very few aircraft on any one base obviously would push operating and maintenance costs beyond politically realistic levels.* More limited dispersal might help, but the costs to the Soviets to counteravail such dispersal through the simple expedient of retargeting more nuclear launchers would undoubtedly be far

---

*We are addressing dispersal in normal peacetime mode here. Obviously, wide dispersal might be worked out economically for crisis situations or if a warning were given. But, as we have argued, to base a posture upon the assumption of adequate warning (or upon the West reacting adequately and in timely fashion to warning signals) is a long-standing critical vulnerability. Dispersal "upon warning" is not a satisfactory solution.

less than the costs to NATO. (This is particularly so given the possibility of hundreds of SS-20 MIRVed warheads by the early 1980s.) So while some degree of dispersal could be effected, there are clear limits to what could be accomplished short of a major change in the role of air power.

A similar situation probably prevails for key C^3 facilities, although much could be done by increasing their mobility, decentralization, redundancy of links, and multiplicity of types of links. Moreover, there is no valid excuse for having the concentrated, unhardened, and undefended facilities as now exist.

While, in principle, it would appear more convenient and far less costly to multiply the number of nuclear warhead storage sites, as contrasted with multiplying air bases, this is politically difficult given concern over peacetime security, which has been increasing and has become a major factor in congressional moves to reduce the weapons deployed in Europe.

Nor is it practical, with existing levels and geographical dispositions of ground forces, to dispense entirely with the present caserne structure. The major casernes cannot readily be broken up and dispersed without incurring major cost increases. To place NATO's ground forces into a dispersed, mobile mode during peacetime would push expenditures well beyond the present level and beyond anything that NATO is prepared to fund. Plainly, if such steps were to be taken, a sharply reduced overall force level is implied, as well as reposturing of national force elements and a new doctrine of defense.

There are all major postural liabilities, particularly if the threat assumed for planning purposes is the one described by Soviet-Pact doctrine. What is required, following changes in doctrine, is a revamped posture as free of such critical drawbacks as possible.

Even if it is unrealistic to expect major improvements in all of these vulnerabilities, this should not preclude efforts to improve some of them. The vulnerability of air assets is a weakness that particularly deserves immediate attention. Quite possibly the role of manned aircraft could be at least as important for a nuclear battlefield as for conventional operations. We are not arguing to do away with aircraft by any means. The critical necessity to acquire, assess, and attack targets quickly in a highly fluid combat situation, where many vital targets are beyond surface acquisition (or satellite observation) capabilities, emphasizes the air role. A rapid recce-evaluation-attack system, which can cope with mobile enemy units over the depth of the battlefield, is of the highest priority. But this also poses a most difficult deployment requirements problem.

Because of their vulnerability to nuclear attack, current NATO nuclear-capable aircraft cannot be depended upon to survive to fulfill this critical role. Clearly what is needed is a class of aircraft that can be dispersed and concealed to thwart Soviet attack objectives. In other words, we are concerned here with the so-called VTOL (vertical take-off and landing) and STOL (short take-off and landing) aircraft.

At present, VTOL technology has not advanced to the point where sufficient range and endurance exist to provide a realistic combat capability for fixed-wing aircraft. More promising for this role would be something along the lines of the Air Force's A-10 fighter-bomber, which can operate from unprepared strips (or even use the rural roadwork) as short as 1000 feet and can perform battlefield reconnaissance for as much as an hour at a radius of 150 miles. One can envisage aircraft of this type roaming over the battlefield area equipped with an array of target sensors—radar, infrared devices, optical devices, and so on—and armed with a number of small, high-velocity air-to-surface missiles that can quickly be delivered on mobile targets before they have had a chance to redispose themselves to reduce the effectiveness of the attack.

As an alternative, or a supplement, to the employment of jet aircraft, high-performance helicopters—having characteristics comparable to the Army's ill-fated Cheyenne—might be an attractive possibility. The lightness of the nuclear payload, as compared with conventional payload requirements, lends to the possibility for extended-range (comparable to, or even greater than, fixed-wing aircraft of the A-10 variety) helicopter operations. And, of course, helicopters have the advantage of true VTOL capabilities, thereby providing a greater degree of survivability than that for dispersed fixed-wing aircraft.

Regarding the vulnerability of the present limited number of nuclear storage sites to nuclear attack, for reasons similar to the issue of U.S. ICBM survivability it is most doubtful that the problem can be overcome by increasing the physical hardness of these sites. The demand for peacetime nuclear warhead security (however excessive and politically motivated it may be) not only seems to preclude an even larger number of dispersed stockpile sites but may also result in further reduction in the present number of sites.

What might be an attractive solution, in part, is a different warhead technology that, in effect, "denuclearizes" the warhead so that the normally associated security problems no longer apply. Two approaches seem promising: (1) utilizing advanced warhead security technologies that substantially reduce the possibility of intact capture or unauthorized use; or (2) adopting the expedient of separating the fissile material from the warhead, so that capture of one of the components does not directly lead to possession of an intact nuclear explosive.

The first approach would appear in principle to satisfy more stringent security requirements, although it would entail considerable additional costs and logistics-handling problems. Also, since the issue of peacetime security and control is largely emotional and political, it is doubtful that those measures alone would enable the wider dispersal necessary to enhance survivability against attack.

The second approach would involve a nuclear capsule stored separately, and perhaps at some distance, from the remainder of the warhead, which would be kept integral with the delivery weapon system. Through such a separation of components, the security issue is placed in a much different perspective. The prospect is no longer that a terrorist or guerrilla team overruns a site and steals one or more intact warheads; rather, the problem at most is one of the theft of either the fissile capsule or the delivery unit (the latter a most difficult task considering the size and weight of most units along with associated launching equipment), or both simultaneously at separate points (to which would be added the probability that the capsule and the delivery unit would not match). As for unauthorized release, complicity would now be required between the units in custody of the capsules and those manning the delivery systems, the possibility of which seems remote at best.

As for the problem of troop and caserne concentration, it is clear that to achieve survivability for these forces through a much more dispersed deployment calls for a significant reduction in the levels of forces presently based in casernes. The question then becomes fundamentally one of what force levels are called for to provide an adequate tactical nuclear defense.

It can be argued that the answer to that question depends upon an understanding of tactical nuclear warfare that no one can have. Without pretending to any such prescience, the fundamental differences in energy release between nuclear and chemical explosives lead to pragmatically logical conclusions. Whatever the required conventional defense to cope with a Pact conventional assault (and were a nuclear attack the one anticipated, then clearly there would be no reason to be concerned with conventional defense!), the force requirements for a defense based upon the application of nuclear firepower would be far below those conforming to conventional defense. Simply put, the fact is that a nuclear warhead weighing on the order of one hundred pounds can have the battlefield effectiveness of tens, or hundreds, or even thousands of tons of high explosive ordnance, depending upon the nature of the target. And changing planning now based upon a lengthy conventional war scenario would free, or lessen the need for, certain force elements required by such a scenario: extended North Atlantic supply lines, extensive stocks of materiel, sizable reserves, and the requirements for massive conventional armaments and attendant manpower levels on the battlefield.

Relying on analysts recently in the office of Secretary of Defense, the Brookings Institution projected the costs of four alternative general purpose force postures: the present posture, reduced forces in Asia, reduced forces in Asia and Europe, and predominant reliance on nuclear weapons. Projected from 1974 to 1980, the annual average costs of these forces in billions of dollars were, respectively: 56.2, 52, 45.7, and 30.[107] In other words, the average annual cost of the nuclear emphasis posture over seven years would be close to one-half less that of the present posture and about two-thirds that of the next cheapest option studied. By 1980, the differences projected would be even starker, the nuclear emphasis posture costing $20 billion per annum compared with $57.5 billion for the present posture. And, we have already referred to the reference to a cheaper posture emphasizing tactical nuclear weapons in the annual Department of Defense report.

Whatever the validity of these precise figures, or the reasonableness of the postulated postures, the suggestion is clear that nuclear-oriented postures can cost considerably less than those with a nonnuclear emphasis. (Note that we are not casting this as nuclear *or* nonnuclear in terms of arms or forces, but in terms of posture and doctrinal emphasis.)

(It can be posited that, were the Soviets to observe a NATO shift to a tactical nuclear emphasis force, including early defensive use of TNW, they would be forced to a more dispersed attack mode avoiding concentration of forces. In that case, the effectiveness of conventional forces might be substantially enhanced.)

Finally, regarding preferred nuclear delivery systems for a new posture, in addition to the aircraft already discussed, and the retention of some artillery (improved mobility), highly mobile, short-range surface-to-surface missiles seem optimum. Ideally, these would incorporate some forms of terminal guidance to increase accuracy, to the extent that is practical and economic. (We would not suggest terminal guidance at a large increase in the unit cost, or for the entire force, since the potential cheapness of such a system and hence the deployable numbers practical are two of its most attractive features.) One could envision two classes of such missiles: (1) those having ranges up to a few tens of miles, and (2) those reaching out beyond the range of aircraft operations to reach beyond the battlefield or to reach into the battlefield from deployment outside it. Basing the design of these missiles on nuclear payloads alone, very lightweight and small missiles can be developed. The shorter-range missiles might weigh a few hundred pounds, according to preliminary technological analysis, about one-tenth that of the Honest John; and the longer-range missile might weigh on the order of a thousand pounds, about one-tenth that of Pershing.

Conclusions

Neither a viable posture nor a viable doctrine exist in NATO for the defense of Europe or more particularly for the employment of tactical nuclear weapons. There are as yet no agreed operational plans for controlling the use of TNW to enhance denial of the objectives of a Pact attack or to hold collateral damage to tolerable levels in the event of large-scale use. Modernization of posture, doctrine, and weapons has been deliberately retarded by insistence of policymakers on planning on a massive Pact *nonnuclear* attack, presaged by long warning lead-time, rather than the real threat vividly evidenced in Soviet doctrine, Pact exercises, and Pact training. Underpinning this apparent belief in the unilateral ability of the West to keep a European conflict non-nuclear is both a persistent divorcing of deterrence from nuclear war-fighting and denial capabilities and a persistent disregard of the fact that the nuclear decision is really up to the Soviets. In response to this, it would be good to repeat at some length the conclusions of three perceptive experts on the Soviet view of warfare:

> *The basic purpose of Soviet nuclear forces, as explained in Soviet sources, is to provide the Soviet Union with a war-fighting and war-winning capability. Soviet doctrine and military posture do not distinguish between deterrent and war-fighting capabilities....*
>
> *Meanwhile, Soviet authorities leave no doubt of their intended reliance on nuclear weapons if a general war should come, whatever its origins.*

> *All Soviet literature and statements dealing with Soviet military capabilities and Soviet strategy uniformly stress the central role that nuclear weapons and, more particularly, nuclear rocket weapons have been assigned in all phases of Soviet military planning and preparations. Importance continues to be attached to conventional weapons, though not as a substitute for, but as a supplement to, nuclear rocket weapons. The furthest that any spokesman has gone with respect to reliance on conventional weapons is to concede that "along with" the nuclear weapons which "will be the main and decisive means of waging conflict," such weapons "will also find use and, in certain circumstances, units and subunits might conduct combat actions with only conventional weapons."*
>
> *Soviet commentators, it should be noted, insist that war in the nuclear age has not ceased to be an instrument of politics, "as is claimed by the overwhelming majority of representatives of pacifist, anti-war movements in the bourgeois world."*[108]

The way out of this problem is not to reemphasize strategic nuclear guarantees, however much Western European allies continue to insist upon the U.S. strategic nuclear guarantee as a sort of *deus ex machina*. The United States may not be able for the foreseeable future to extricate itself from these strategic force guarantees,* even ultimately the threat of a strategic exchange with the USSR over Europe, and we stop short of suggesting that the United States should. However, it is no longer reasonable or prudent to *rely* on such "coupling" of strategic retaliatory forces to the theater as we have in the past, as has been officially recognized:

> *It is a different decision for the President of the United States to risk general nuclear war when the strategic equation is less than it was throughout most of the postwar period. Therefore, the possibility of defending other countries with strategic American power alone has fundamentally changed, and no amount of reassurance on our part can change these facts.*[109]
>
> *During the 1970s, the Soviets achieved overall parity in strategic forces with the United States. The threat of mutual annihilation limits the range of hostile actions which can be deterred by strategic forces and places more emphasis on the deterrent roles of theater nuclear and conventional forces.*

---

*"So long as Western Europe is not an effective and united nuclear power in its own right, such a hope [strategic decoupling] is unrealistic. If the United States intends to participate in maintaining the security of Western Europe, she must be willing to face an ultimate strategic nuclear showdown or recognize, if only privately, that her policy in Europe is a bluff that can be called by a truly resolute nuclear opponent." Laurence Martin, "Theater Nuclear Weapons and Europe," *Survival* 16 (November/December, 1974), p. 273.

Such escalation [to general nuclear exchanges] would not be in the interest of either the United States or its European allies, nor the WP for that matter.[110]

Seemingly ingrained European resistance to a TNW emphasis strategy is based upon a complex of perceptions and misperceptions—political, economic, and nuclear, including that of collateral damage. The critical matter remains that of the nature of the threat. Neither Soviet nor American nuclear warheads nor their likely employment necessarily lead to the conclusion of large-scale collateral damage; serious analysis of both, in fact, tends toward the opposite possibility,* at least if steps are taken by the West to enhance the discriminate nature of its TNW as we are technically and operationally capable of doing.

Whether or not an initially limited TNW conflict in Europe will escalate to general war proportions or to strategic exchanges is a matter of pure conjecture, but it is not unrelated to policy, plans and military considerations. The presumption that such a process is somehow inevitable, or occurs because each side feels it can achieve military advantages in ascending the escalator in that direction has little foundation, empirically or logically, and even less if we posture ourselves so as not to rely on strategies of escalation even in the face of a nuclear threat. In fact, to assume that the United States is committed to such coupling, or that the Soviets will refrain from theater nuclear usage for fear of it, is erroneous.

Recognition of the vulnerabilities in our NATO posture and the weaknesses in our TNW planning and doctrine does not imply the ability to carry through necessary reforms. Unlike the strategic force arena, where the matter is up to the United States alone, perception of problems and moves to correct them must be on the basis of agreement multilaterally within an Alliance with some diversity of views and priorities. This is particularly so given the fact that the type of meaningful changes espoused here would require rather far-reaching departures in thinking, planning, and posturing from those that exist. Still, it is imperative that the United States take the lead in dialogue and movement toward them.

*Elsewhere the authors have examined possible ways of alleviating the collateral damage problem even further. S. T. Cohen and W. R. Van Cleave, "Western European Collateral Damage and Tactical Nuclear Weapons," *RUSI* (Journal of Royal United Services Institute), June 1976.

Tactical Nuclear Weapons: an Examination of the Issues

S. T. Cohen and William R. Van Cleave

References

1. U. S., Department of Defense, *The Theater Nuclear Force Posture in Europe*, A report to the United States Congress in compliance with Public Law 93-365, April 1, 1975.
2. Vannevar Bush, *Modern Arms and Free Men* (New York: Simon and Schuster, 1949), pp. 106-107. The editor of the *Bulletin of the Atomic Scientists*, Eugene Rabinowitch, wrote in 1952 that "I would say this development—the shift of atomic weapons from mass destruction to limited objectives—is the only one that scientists did not foresee in 1945. Scientists did not anticipate a possibility that atomic weapons would be used mainly for tactical purposes." ("An Interview with Senator Mc-Mahon," Bulletin of the Atomic Scientists 8 [January 1952]: 10.)
3. Edward Teller with Allen Brown, *The Legacy of Hiroshima* (New York: Doubleday, 1962), p. 31.
4. Cited in George C. Reinhardt, *Nuclear Weapons and Limited Warfare: A Sketchbook History*, P-3022 (Santa Monica, Calif.: Rand Corporation, November 1964): 4.
5. Gordon Dean, *Report on the Atom* (New York: Alfred A. Knopf, 1953), p. 73.
6. "News Conference Statement by Secretary Dulles," *Department of State Bulletin* 32 (January 3, 1955): 13-14.
7. Alain C. Enthoven and K. Wayne Smith, *How Much Is Enough: Shaping the Defense Program 1961-1969* (New York: Harper & Row, 1971), p. 117.
8. This information on army training, the CGSC curriculum, the contents

of the journal *Military Review,* and the quotations of army directives is taken from a recent Ph.D. dissertation by John P. Rose, Major, U.S. Army, "U.S. Army Doctrinal Developments: The Nuclear Battlefield, 1945–1977," University of Southern California, School of International Relations, Defense and Strategic Studies Program, 1977.

9. Ibid., chap. 4.

10. Michael A. Molino, Major, U.S. Army, "Division Defensive Operations for Nuclear and Nonnuclear Environments," *Military Review,* December 1973. Cited in Rose, "U.S. Army Doctrinal Developments."

11. U. S., President, *Public Papers of the Presidents of the United States* (Washington, D.C.: Office of the *Federal Register,* National Archives and Records Service, 1965), Lyndon B. Johnson, 2, July 1 to December 31, 1964, p. 1051.

12. U. S. Department of Defense, *Report of the Secretary of Defense James R. Schlesinger to the Congress on the FY 1975 Defense Budget and FY 1975-1979 Defense Program* (Washington, D.C.: Government Printing Office, 1974), p. 82.

13. Letter to Senator John Stennis from President Jimmy Carter, July 11, 1977.

14. J. Robert Oppenheimer, "Comments on the Military Value of the Atom," *Bulletin of the Atomic Scientists* 7 (February 1951): 44-45.

15. *NATO and the New Soviet Threat,* Report of Senator Sam Nunn and Senator Dewey F. Bartlett to the Committee on Armed Services, United States Senate, January 24, 1977. (Washington, D.C.: Government Printing Office, 1977).

16. Joint Chiefs of Staff, *Dictionary of Military and Associated Terms,* Department of Defense, JCS Pub, 1, Washington, D.C., September 1974, pp. 314, 326.

17. Edward B. Giller (Lieutenant General USAF, retired), "Tomorrow's Strategic Options," Address to Air Force Association, Vandenberg AFB, California, 1976, as represented in *ERDA News,* June 1976, pp. 6-7.

18. James R. Schlesinger, "Organizational Structures and Planning," in *Issues in Defense Economics,* ed. Roland N. McKean (New York: Columbia University Press, 1967), p. 209.

19. Department of Defense, *FY 1975 Defense Budget.* Page numbers in parentheses.

20. Ibid., p. 82.

21. Secretary of Defense Donald H. Rumsfeld, *Annual Defense Department Report, FY 1977,* January 27, 1976, pp. 80-85, 88 ff.

22. Secretary of Defense Donald H. Rumsfeld, *Annual Defense Department Report, FY 1978,* January 17, 1977, p. 118 (and p. 147 for specific improvements deemed necessary).

23. Henry A. Kissinger, *The Troubled Partnership* (New York: McGraw-Hill, 1965), p. 180.
24. U. S. Department of Defense, *Report of Secretary of Defense James R. Schlesinger to the Congress on the FY 1976 and Transition Budgets, FY 1977 Authorization Request and FY 1976-1980 Defense Programs* (Washington, D.C.: Government Printing Office, 1975), pp. iii-1.
25. Dr. Fred C. Iklé, Address to Town Hall of California, Los Angeles, August 31, 1976. U.S. Arms Control and Disarmament Agency, Washington, D.C.
26. Andrei A. Grechko, *On Guard for Peace and the Building of Communism*, trans. Joint Publications Research Service (Springfield, Va.: National Technical Information Service, 1972; first published in Moscow in 1971), p. 33.
27. A. A. Sidorenko, *The Offensive*, trans. under the auspices of the U. S. Air Force (Washington, D.C.: Government Printing Office, 1974; first published in Moscow in 1970), p. 221. The Pentagon's response to the Nunn amendment states: "For a Soviet exposition of this strategy and doctrine see, for example, A. A. Sidorenko, *The Offensive*." (U. S. Department of Defense, *The Theater Nuclear Force Posture in Europe*, p. 9n.)
28. Hearings, Military Procurement Authorization, FY 1964, p. 29.
29. John Foster Dulles, "Challenge and Response in United States Policy," *Foreign Affairs* 26 (October 1957), p. 31.
30. J. E. Campbell and H. A. Sandmaier, *Radiation Transport in Air Over Ground and Air Over Seawater for Application to Low-Altitude, Low-Yield Tactical Nuclear Detonations*, NWEF Report 1102 (Albuquerque, N.M.: Naval Weapons Evaluation Facility, 1973). See also Senator Gaylord Nelson, "Report on Tactical Nuclear Weapons," Congressional Record, July 20, 1971, pp. 26163-6; Colonel René David, "La Bombe à neutrons: mythe ou réalité?" *Défense Nationale* (Paris) 28 (July 1972): 1160-73; and Robert M. Lawrence, "On Tactical Nuclear War," Revue Militaire Générale (Paris), February 1971, p. 243.
31. Captain Arnold S. Warshawsky, USA, "Radiation Battlefield Casualties —Credible!" *Military Review* 56, 5 (May 1976): 5; and 8.
32. Major General G. Biryukov and Colonel G. Melnikov, *Antitank Warfare* (Moscow: Progress Publishers, 1972), p. 69.
33. Freeman Dyson, "The Future Development of Nuclear Weapons," *Foreign Affairs* 38 (April 1960): 457-464.
34. Communication from Adrian S. Fisher to Senator Thomas A. Dodd, March 14, 1963, *Congressional Record*, April 9, 1963, p. 5986.
35. Frank Carey, "U. S. Discloses Its Weapons in Nuclear Arsenal," *Los Angeles Times*, September 6, 1967, pp. 1-17.

36. *Public Works for Water and Power Development and Energy Research Appropriation Bill*, 1978. Hearings before the Subcommittee on Public Works, U.S. House of Representatives, March 17, 1977, p. 1089.

37. Sidorenko, *Offensive*, pp. 84, 92.

38. Enthoven and Smith, *How Much Is Enough?* pp. 126-127. Testimony of Dr. Carl Walske, assistant to the secretary of defense for Atomic Energy in the U.S. Congress-Senate Committee on Foreign Relations, *Prospects for Comprehensive Nuclear Test Ban Treaty*. Hearings before the Subcommittee on Arms Control, International Law Organization, 92nd Cong., 1st sess., 1971 (Washington, D.C.: Government Printing Office, 1971), pp. 131-133. Marshal K. Kazakov, *Pod Znamenem Leninizma*, No. 19, October 1972 (JPRS 57799, December 19, 1972).

39. Testimony in U.S., Congress, House, Committee on Appropriations, *Department of Defense Appropriations for 1974*. Hearings before the Subcommittee on the Department of Defense, 93rd Cong., 1st sess., 1973 (Washington, D.C.: Government Printing Office, 1973), p. 197.

40. Giller, "Tomorrow's Strategic Options," p. 7.

41. Communications from Rep. Craig Hosmer to Secretary of Defense Clark Clifford, *Congressional Record*, July 31, 1968, p. 24437.

42. L. A. Artsimovich, "Research on Controlled Thermonuclear Reactions in the U.S.S.R.," *Proceedings of the Second United Nations International Conference on the Peaceful Uses of Atomic Energy* 31 (Geneva: United Nations, 1958).

43. Biryukov and Melnikov, *Antitank Warfare*, p. 69.

44. Department of Defense, *FY 1976 and Transition Budgets*, p. iii-1.

45. Grechko, *On Guard for Peace*, pp. 33, 43.

46. *Ibid.*, p. 43.

47. Sidorenko, *Offensive*, p. 113.

48. *Aviation Week and Space Technology*, August 1, 1977.

49. Giller, "Tomorrow's Strategic Options," p. 7.

50. Cf. Trevor Cliffe, *Military Technology and the European Balance*, Adelphi Papers No. 89 (London: 1155, 1972), pp. 35-36; also any recent Military Balance and annual report of Chairman, Joint Chiefs of Staff.

51. See, for example, U. S., Department of the Army and Department of the Navy, *Staff Officers Field Manual, Nuclear Weapons Employment Doctrine and Procedures* (Washington, D.C.: Government Printing Office, 1968).

52. The Schlesinger quotation is from Department of Defense, *FY 1975 Defense Budget*, p. 82. The Grechko quotation is from *On Guard for Peace*, p. 33. The Shtemenko quotation is cited in P. M. Derevyanko,

ed., *Problems in the Revolution in Military Affairs* (Moscow: Voyenizdat, 1965), p. 83.

53. Field-Marshal the Viscount Montgomery of Alamein, "A Look Through a Window at World War III," *Journal of the Royal United Service Institution* 99 (November 1954): 508.

54. John F. Kennedy, *The Strategy of Peace* (New York: Harper & Row, 1960), p. 185.

55. U. S. President, *U. S. Foreign Policy for the 1970's: The Emerging Structure of Peace, A Report to the Congress by Richard Nixon, February 9, 1972* (Washington, D.C.: Government Printing Office, 1972), p. 43.

56. Testimony in U. S., Congress, Joint Committee on Atomic Energy, *Military Applications of Nuclear Technology.* Hearings before the Subcommittee on Military Applications, Part 2, 93rd Cong., 1st sess., 1973 (Washington, D.C.: Government Printing Office, 1973), pp. 100-101.

57. Department of Defense, *The Theater Nuclear Force Posture in Europe,* p. 14.

58. Department of Defense, *FY 1975 Defense Budget,* p. 81.

59. Testimony of Dr. Carl Walske in *Military Applications of Nuclear Technology,* pp. 36, 40.

60. Testimony in U. S. Congress, Senate, Subcommittee on U. S. Security Agreements and Commitments Abroad of the Committee on Foreign Relations, *Nuclear Weapons and Foreign Policy,* 93rd Cong., 2nd Sess., March 14, 1974, p. 54.

61. Grechko, *On Guard for Peace,* p. 31; and p. 52.

62. Lieutenant General I. Zavyalov, "Nuclear Weapons and War," *Krasnaya Zvezda,* October 30, 1970.

63. Major General I. E. Krupchenko et al., *Military History* (Moscow: Voenigdat, 1971), p. 343.

64. Sidorenko, *Offensive,* p. 115.

65. Chief Marshal of Armored Troops P. A. Rotmistrov, *Vremya: Tanki* (Moscow: Publishing House of the USSR Ministry of Defense, 1972), JPRS translation No. 969, January 1974.

66. Grechko, *On Guard for Peace,* pp. 51-52.

67. Zavyalov, "Nuclear Weapons"; Sidorenko, *Offensive,* p. 49.

68. Krupchenko, *Military History.*

69. Grechko, *On Guard for Peace,* p. 35.

70. Denis Healey, "Thinking About the Unthinkable—Denis Healey, Secretary of State for Defense, Talks to Laurence Martin," *The Listener* (London), April 23, 1970, p. 538.

71. Grechko, *On Guard for Peace,* p. 43.

72. General-Major A. S. Milovidov and Colonel V. G. Kozlov, eds., *The Philosophical Heritage of V. I. Lenin and Problems of Contemporary War.* Translated under the auspices of the U. S. Air Force (Washington, D.C.: Government Printing Office, 1974; first published in Moscow in 1972), pp. 150, 104-105.
73. Zavyalov, "Nuclear Weapons."
74. Rotmistrov, *Vremya: Tanki.*
75. Rear Admiral Professor V. Shelyag, "Two World Outlooks—Two Views on War," *Krasnaya Znezda,* February 7, 1974, Foreign Broadcast Information Service, SQV-74-30, February 12, 1974.
76. Milovidov and Kozlov, *Problems of Contemporary War,* pp. 45-47.
77. John Erickson, *Soviet Military Power,* U. S. Strategic Institute Report 73-1 (Washington, D.C.: U.S. Strategic Institute, 1973), p. 77.
78. Department of Defense, *The Theater Nuclear Force Posture in Europe,* pp. 2, 10, 13.
79. John R. Thomas, "Limited Nuclear War in Soviet Strategic Thinking," *Orbis* 10 (Spring 1966): p. 203.
80. Testimony of James R. Schlesinger in U. S., Congress, Senate, Foreign Relations Committee, *Nuclear Weapons and Foreign Policy.* Hearings before the Subcommittee on United States Security Agreements and Commitments Abroad and the Subcommittee on Arms Control, International Law and Organization, 93rd Cong., 2nd sess., 1974 (Washington, D.C.: Government Printing Office, 1974), p. 183.
81. Grechko, "On Guard Over Peace and Socialism," *Kommunist,* no. 7, May 8, 1973.
82. A. A. Grechko, *The Armed Forces of the Soviet State* (Moscow: Voyenizdat, 1974), p. 275.
83. Benjamin S. Lambeth, "The Sources of Soviet Military Doctrines," in *Comparative Defense Policy,* eds. Frank B. Horton, III, Anthony C. Rogerson, and Edward L. Warner, III (Baltimore, Md.: Johns Hopkins University Press, 1974), p. 214.
84. Department of Defense, *FY 1975 Defense Budget,* pp. 81-82.
85. Grechko, *On Guard for Peace,* pp. 32, 43.
86. Department of Defense, *FY 1975 Defense Budget,* p. 87.
87. Iklé, Address to Town Hall of California.
88. Great Britain, Parliamentary Debate (Commons), vol. 769, July 25, 1968, cols. 1015-1016.
89. Department of Defense, *FY 1975 Defense Budget,* p. 82.
90. *White Paper 1975/1976: The Security of the Federal Republic of Germany and the Development of the Federal Armed Forces,* Ministry of Defense, Government of the Federal Republic of Germany, 1976.

91. Department of Defense, *FY 1975 Defense Budget*, p. 82.

92. *Defense Department Report*, FY 1977, p. 88.

93. William P. Rogers, "Strategic Arms Limitations Tables, Address by Secretary Rogers," *Department of State Bulletin* 61 (December 1, 1969): p. 465.

94. Interview, *U. S. News & World Report*, March 15, 1976.

95. N. I. Krylov, "The Instructive Lessons of History," *Sovietskaya Russia*, August 30, 1969.

96. Paul H. Nitze, "Assuring Strategic Stability in an Era of Detente," *Foreign Affairs* 54, 2 (January 1976): p. 211.

97. Cited in *Los Angeles Times*, October 9, 1974, p. 2.

98. Testimony in *Briefing on Counterforce Attacks*, p. 44.

99. Department of Defense, *FY 1976 and Transition Budgets*, pp. iii-3.

100. Testimony in *Nuclear Weapons and Foreign Policy*, p. 155.

101. Testimony in *Nuclear Weapons and Foreign Policy*, 93rd Cong., 2nd sess., 1974, pp. 62-63.

102. Testimony in *Nuclear Weapons and Foreign Policy*, 93rd Cong., 2nd sess., 1974, pp. 72-74.

103. Testimony in *Nuclear Weapons and Foreign Policy*, 93rd Cong., 2nd sess., 1974, p. 21.

104. Testimony in *Nuclear Weapons and Foreign Policy*, 93rd Cong., 2nd sess., 1974, p. 60.

105. Testimony in *Nuclear Weapons and Foreign Policy*, 93rd Cong., 2nd sess., 1974, p. 8.

106. B.Gen. William F. Train, "The Atomic Challenge," *Military Review*, November 1956. Quoted in John Rose, *ibid.*

107. E. R. Fried, A. M. Rivlin, C. L. Schultze, and N. H. Teeters, *Setting National Priorities* (Washington, D.C.: The Brookings Institution, 1973), pp. 365-373.

108. Leon Goure, Foy Kohler, and Mose Harvey, *The Role of Nuclear Forces in Current Soviet Strategy* (Miami: University of Miami, Center for Advanced International Studies, 1974), pp. 8-10.

109. Henry A. Kissinger, "Background Briefing to the Press," Chicago, Ill., September 16, 1970, mimeographed, p. 10.

110. Department of Defense, *Theater Nuclear Force Posture in Europe*, pp. 1-2, 14.

Index

Index

A-10 fighter-bomber, 96
ADM (atomic demolition munition),
Accuracy of Soviet missiles, 52
AFAP (artillery fired atomic projec-
tile), 14
Air bases, 48-49
Air force, Soviet, 48
Aircraft, 49
    NATO, 96
    VTOL, 96
Antitank guided missiles (ATGMS), 49n
Antitank warfare, Soviet, 34, 43
Armed forces, *See* Conventional forces
Armed Services Committee, U.S. Sen-
ate, 10-11
Arms Control Impact Statement (AIS),
37-38
Army (magazine), 85n
Artisimovich, L.A., 42
Asian-Pacific area, 1
Atomic Energy Commission (AEC),
35-36

B-52 bombers, 90-91
Ballistic rockets and missiles, 49
Bartlett, Dewey, 10-11
Blast effects, 33-34
Blitzkrieg attacks, 86
Brodie, Bernard, 86

Brookings Institution, 98
Bush, Vannevar, 3

C^3 facilities, 94-95
Carter, Jimmy, 8-9, 37-38, 61n, 62, 72
Casernes, 95, 97-98
Central Nervous System (CNS) Syn-
drome, 32, 33
Civilian casualties, enhanced radiation
warheads and, 34-35
Collateral damage, 30-31
Combined arms forces, Soviet, 47-48,
65-67, 70-72
Command and General Staff College
(CGSC), 5-6
Congress, U.S., 1-2
Consultation process in NATO, 58
Conventional defense, 2
Conventional forces in Soviet doctrine
and strategy, 65-67, 70-73
    training for nuclear combat, 93-94
    U.S.-NATO doctrine on, 60
Cotter, D.R., 78n

Dean, Gordon, 4
Defense Department
    reports on tactical nuclear weapons,
    18-20, 23
    tactical and strategic nuclear weapons
    as defined by, 13-15